Persecuted, But Not Forsaken

How God uses your Devastation on your way to your Destination

Memoirs of a Survivor

Onica Michelle Royal

For Randy my epitomized strength forever loved

This book is protected by the copyright laws of the United States of America. This book may not be copied or reprinted for commercial gain or profit. No part of this publication may be reproduced, distributed, or transmitted in any form or by any means or stored in a database or retrieval system without prior written permission of the Publisher.

Copyright # 1-7189582591
ISBN: 978-0-578-42672-3

Copyright ©2020 Onica Michelle Royal
All rights reserved, including the right to reproduce this book or portion thereof in any form whatsoever. Contact email is Kingdomconcepts2018@gmail.com

Table of Contents

Preface 5

Chapter 1: Treasure in Earthen Vessels 4:7 7

Chapter 2: There Is Liberty 3:17 13

Chapter 3: By Faith 5:7 17

Chapter 4: Things Seen Are Temporal 4:18 25

Chapter 5: The Promises of God 1:20 37

Chapter 6: Lest Satan Should Get an Advantage 2:10-11 47

Chapter 7: Perfect in Weakness 12:9 57

Chapter 8: This Thorn 12:7 75

Chapter 9: Causing Us to Triumph 2:14 93

About the Author 99

Preface

Embedded within the pages of this journal are a series of journeys of sorts that depict how a sovereign God can take pain and trade it for purpose. For every why there's a "because" and for every question, there is an answer. Situations, people, problems, and processes are all necessary for the tumultuous hike to your destiny. The downfalls, the detours, the long, dark, seemingly endless winding roads that foreshadow a place called Nowhere are all imperative for the process.

To believe that we serve a God that intentionally created *living* purpose within each of us, one that is divinely and uniquely shaped, will then have this same *living* purpose become useless, wither away and perish is folly! God in His divine wisdom intends to get a return for all that He has invested in each of us. II Corinthians 4:7 reminds, "But we have this treasure in earthen vessels, that the excellency of the power may be of God, and not of us." If you are faithful and willing to endure the process, God will take your moments of devastation and transform them into platforms, useful and vital for your ultimate destination.

The basis for this book is founded upon the words of the Apostle Paul, who himself became familiarly acquainted with many hardships, tests, and trials. Each chapter is based upon his words in II Corinthians 4:8-9, which ultimately is the lot of every blood-bought believer where he imparts, "We are troubled on every side, yet not distressed; we are perplexed, but not in despair; **Persecuted, but not forsaken**; cast down, but not destroyed."

Here between vagueness and victory is where the passage of your purpose begins! When there's nothing left to grasp but the impossible, God extends His loving hand to lead—from Devastation to Destiny. Take the ride! Enjoy the vast scenery, learn from the pit stops, but never, ever stop moving forward! There's much to be discovered in this journey of YOU!

Chapter 1

𝔗reasure in 𝔈arthen 𝔙essels 4:7

"But this beautiful treasure is contained in us—cracked pots made of earth and clay so that the transcendent character of this power will be clearly seen as coming from God and not from us."

    If only Mona Lisa could speak, I wonder exactly the weight of the words that would escape from behind that priceless smile. Would she excite you with the story of a journey that led her to be captured in the timeless work of art by DaVinci? Would there be tales of extremely blissful moments of happiness or tragic recollections of wounds from times past? Like my own, her smile shares only *one* version of her story, the one everyone thinks they know, while her eyes posing as the windows to her soul expose the truth. Who would dare have the courage to trespass beyond the fortified walls of her self-protected, introverted being? They had purposely been erected to keep at bay those who came to rescind her divine assignment. The empty space behind the walls of my soul only gave the impression to house countless ranks of consuming darkness that seemed to be clustered as one perpetual, lifeless abyss! This darkness so thick and blinding at times was unpredictably scary. It seemed the only solution was to invoke darkness' most effective antidote—the illuminating light of God's Word.

    In the same way much like Mona Lisa, I've been recognized and known for my smile. Somehow through the horrendous muck and mire, I have always managed to regularly keep one. Most times it had been plastered upon my face to mirror the condition of the heart I'd always longed for; the one I dreamed of one day conceiving, one that wasn't damaged, calloused, or cold. This smile that I wore amazingly was just as resilient as the wounded spirit I housed inside this battle-scarred frame.

Unless you were an astute historian you wouldn't know what brought Mona Lisa to be chosen to display her enduring expression but I have come to realize that my smile is a testament of strength and God-given grace. This smile would be the constant reminder that it wasn't merely formed by muscles and tendons that respond to reflexes and external stimuli, it was fashioned, formed, and made manifest by the skillful Creator who would use it for His glory!

I am only one individual of many, nothing extraordinarily significant, with meager beginnings and no substantial evidence to prove I was destined to be here, I felt. From the beginning I was chosen. From the start I was blessed, but could not fathom the circumstances and life-altering events from which all of these things God had pre-ordained would be extracted.

It seems that right from the beginning, the enemy launched a horrific attack to ambush, annihilate, and destroy my life. Like a target isolated on a gun range, the one I invisibly wore was only visible to my enemies. Their weapons were formed and initially I knew this quite well. But what exactly the weaponry would entail and how effective each article of artillery would become, I did not yet know. Time and countless trials would be the most accurate historians of how one could endure incidences of persecution, yet remain confident in the fact that I had not one incident of ever being forsaken by God.

Being a daddy's girl and one of his faithful traveling companions, our relationship was unbreakable and in my eyes my father could do no wrong. I trusted him and hung onto his every word, especially whenever we would hold our many conversations while trekking endless roads either before or immediately after he'd exerted acts of ministry. If I had learned a new word or caught a new catch phrase I'd be sure to ask him the meaning. After some sermons I witnessed him preach, I would recap the information during our talks on the way home. I asked him questions about the

Bible and subjects I was unsure about and he excitedly supplied answers, every single time. He never missed an opportunity to pour knowledge and wisdom into me. Moreover, it thrilled him to see my thirst and zeal to learn new things. He'd never given me a reason to doubt or second-guess anything he said. Every question had a valid answer when it came to him. Except this one conversation we had. I was around the age of 4 and there were just five little words spoken that abruptly altered the trajectory of my innocent young life. Trying to comprehend where I came from and why I was born, why my friends had both a mom and a dad and I only had a dad, I needed to know what purpose I served by being here with what I assumed was a disadvantage. From this moment forward, my soul, the meaning of all living things and the reason why they existed, became drastically malformed. My fragile spirit, yearning to understand as well as be understood, hearkened unto these alarming words spoken by him that I was unprepared for, "No. You were NOT planned."

It was spoken emphatically and without emotion. *What?! Oh, my God! That just couldn't be right*, I thought. How could that be the truth when God declared from the beginning that everything He made was *good* and made with intentional purpose? I was devastated and completely torn! No mistake about it, I heard the words clearly and what I interpreted them to mean was, *No. You were never meant to be here. No. You were not wanted. No. There is no purpose for you.*

He meant no ill intent and couldn't discern how crushing these words were to an immature, inferior, and insignificant being as I now thought myself to be, trying to discover my place in this cruel, haunting world. It would be a long while before the world would vaguely show signs of its acceptance of me.

To begin, my social history was comprised of my mother, who was the product of a strict father shaped and bred out of the military and an assiduous mother who in a bizarre winter storm accident tragically lost her life while attempting to cross a busy city street. Mama was only 16 years old when a huge portion of her world suddenly changed and normalcy as she knew it ceased. Without permission or proper notice, this unforeseen event occurred and took hostage of the comforting life she had become accustomed to. At a very impressionable time in her life, this single event would have lasting effects that would subtly play out throughout her life, but for a time she was able to hold strong to the faith her grandmother spoke of and relied heavily upon the support system made up of family and close friends.

From recollection, so was the story of my father. He was the product of a strong, God-fearing, Christian mother and a military father. His father fought a tour of the Korean War. When he returned from war, Daddy's father became ill and spent a significant amount of time in the hospital. Because the illness had become so severe and treatment had failed, he later died and left a young faithful wife and six small children behind, yet to be raised. My father being only 5-years-old at the time and second to the oldest, a young boy not fully able to understand the finality and concept of death, built his strength and understanding of God's Word, grace, and peace upon the fundamental teachings of his mother, Louise, and his favorite, most talked about pastor, the Rev. W. W. Wilson.

Indeed, my parents had plenty in common and could readily relate to the deep hurts that life sometimes dealt and both were able to recall to memory all of its unfortunate losses. As high school sweethearts they found comfort in each other's presence. And maybe the tragedies are what brought them together--maybe the unbridled pain was the catalyst that would ultimately tear them apart. When hurt marries hurt, without utilizing the proper processes of healing, it begets more hurt.

Life was beginning to show me that quite possibly I was birthed in the midst of, and maybe because of, hurt. This explains how I inherited such intense circumstances of pain throughout my own life. Nevertheless, love has proven to be the most powerful and most beautiful thing! Is this why God chose to be embodied with it, so much so that He called Himself LOVE?

Regardless, no matter how a thing begins, whether good, bad, or ugly, God is able to fashion and form it beautifully through perfect love. His only son, Jesus, is a prime example. Jesus' death was a gruesome one and, at first thought, nothing beautiful could have been imagined to emerge from such brutality and injustice. Yet God, through His infinite wisdom, saw that this sacrifice, His Son, would be the *only* way to establish a perfect love between Himself and humanity; one that could never be denied or erased.

I never understood why I always had the need to love others with such intensity, until I realized that I possessed the desire and the longing to *be* loved with that same intensity. Until I was introduced to the all-consuming love that Christ provides, I had never known a love so encompassing, not even close in comparison either in word or deed. Although this journey of love has no ending, it has many pit stops that teach countless pleasant and sometimes gut-wrenching lessons.

My father often shared the story of my birth and how I was challenged, even at my arrival into the world. Not only was he one of the first greeters to welcome me, health complications stood nearby. I was slightly underdeveloped and placed into an incubator for a couple of weeks until I became well enough to be discharged. Was I already not enough to endure this world according to its standards? Time would tell.

For a long time the magnitude of the treasures that God had placed inside of me lay quiet and dormant and even somewhat hidden from the creation HE formed to house it—me! Many unfortunate events would come blowing into my life that attempted to hurl me off course and to weaken the power of my voice. Most of the time, the vile tactics proved to be effective temporarily, only because I hadn't utilized The Handbook that would guide and change my life and teach me who and whose I was. But one thing is sure, valued treasures cannot stay hidden forever, especially when a sovereign God and HIS plan are in operation. These treasures are only truly valued when it escapes obscurity and is found by its owner, who then dotes on it and adorns it for HIS pleasure. The value placed on the treasure is a matter of the heart and the owner knowing that its significance and worth could not easily be replaced, if at all.

Given the early prognosis and complications of my birth it was easy to see that the cards were already stacked against me and that seemingly I would have to become satisfied with the heaps of falsehood the enemy attempted to force-feed me about my worth. One by one God would prove diligent in purging every lie of Satan that I had readily digested and made me understand what it is to walk in true purpose.

Chapter 2

There Is Liberty 3:17

"Now the Lord is that Spirit; and where the Spirit of the Lord *is*, there *is* liberty."

    My earliest recollection of initially understanding God's love for me happened at the age of 9. Nine seems like such a tender age in retrospect; a time in which things seemed so pure and undefiled. Nevertheless, the experiences I fought through by this age made me mentally and intellectually appear so much older than I actually was. Confused about *who* I was and *how* my existence could potentially be of any significance to anyone this side of Heaven, I remained guarded and suspecting of others due to the constant, inner mental debates of being loved and to what degree, when life showed me that I was barely *liked*, at most, tolerated.

    Early on in life I knew that I was *different*, but coming to accept this fact took me on an eventful journey that I did not sign up for nor anticipated. Indeed the trek was a treacherous and tedious one. It was apparent that I had the same number of extremities that I saw those around me with. And, at times, I even had nearly the same abilities and skill set. My laugh wasn't exactly a distinct one, neither was my cry, but I sensed deep down on the inside that I possessed something unique and extraordinarily special that I could never detect symmetrically in those around me. Throughout my life I've even met others that discerned what I had, but they couldn't quite describe the weight of it or place their finger upon it. Oh, and how ecstatic I was to discover that this "it" was placed on the *inside* of me, somewhere no one could touch "it," take "it" away, misuse "it," or abuse "it"! Tucked safely away, and at the same time earnestly waiting to break forth, it's something that sadly only a few find in this life, but everyone has—a purpose and a gift from God.

I remember so vividly that one particular night before I had gone asleep, God allowed me to see a vision. This was no ordinary vision where the average 9-year-old imagines possessing the latest gadgets or become overly obsessed with Barbie and Ken's future goals. This was a life-altering experience that only the presence of God gives to His children. Although He had visited me several times by this point, each encounter was a building block for what He previously had shown me. I recognized His voice so well. This night, I lay still in the bed, on my back with my face toward Heaven and I listened. My spirit was at attention and I discerned that I would be given distinct instructions. And I listened.

Gradually, God began to unfold His plans for my life. I recalled He appeared as an intense, illuminating light that sat on a high throne and I was ushered from Earth to Glory in seconds. As God called me by name, I stood before Him and His throne, earnestly waiting to approach Him. As my name left His mouth, the Spirit led me up a brightly lit flight of stairs that ascended to His throne. God's countenance was so blindingly bright that I could not see His face. He held out His hand as I stood. God's loving presence confirmed that it was OK to move forward. He led me up onto His lap and I quietly sat. He said, "ONICA? I NEED YOU TO DO SOMETHING IMPORTANT FOR ME. WILL YOU DO IT?" "Yes…," I replied, affirming what my spirit felt. "YOU ARE CHOSEN AND I WANT YOU TO SPEAK FOR ME."

Without saying another word, I nodded and suddenly He lifted me up from HIS lap, led me down the stairs that were before His throne, and just as I had been in Heaven with God to hear His Word over my life, my foot touched Earth again and, instantly, I was free! My heart was made glad because that one word from God had freed me forever! This experience was indescribable and cannot adequately be put into words that would convey the weightiness of it. I could not make sleep call my name that night. I felt the love of God like I had never experienced it before. How could a great and powerful God require me to do something for Him? Who was I that He would be mindful of me? My heart leapt, my mind raced, my spirit rejoiced! God wanted *me* to speak for Him.

There was only one problem, though—I didn't have a voice! Who knew *freedom* was so short-lived and *forever* was such a short span of time? Here, the enemy taunted me and prodded me to deny and doubt every word that the Lord had just spoken simply because my circumstances did not line up with what He foreknew and declared over my life. Indeed, the assignment was great; I just hadn't learned yet that God was greater.

By this season in my life, my spirit was torn down and raggedy. Through no fault of my own, but by the hands of those propelled as agents of the enemy to deter and destroy God's plans for my life. Isn't it amazing how God will solicit you to do something that you know can't happen in your own strength? Of course, God wouldn't ask you to do what He knows you can perform for yourself! He gives instructions to accomplish those things He knows you will have to lean and depend solely on Him to complete! This is why we walk in faith *with* Him, because it is a journey of trust and exchanging our wills for His perfect will. Without Him and without His guidance, we can truly do nothing.

The Bible declares that many are called, but few are chosen. Chosen means not among the ordinary, but rather original and unique. I'd been searched out among many, but still had been declared as being one-of-a-kind.

All throughout the Bible rests countless subjects from different backgrounds, enduring horrendous obstacles that eventually gave all glory back to their God. I am them; they are me. Consistently gleaning from their faith and confidence in God and how they faced challenging times, people, and situations gave me the blueprint to stay the course of my own faith journey.

Did I start and fail at times just as they had? Of course! Did I learn from my mistakes? Did I get up and run again? Of course! Being bound and imprisoned in my mind, body, and spirit due to the endless attacks of Satan caused me to seek the freedom I needed outside of myself and find it solely in Him. The renewed feelings of a newly- released inmate just arriving home that has had to endure countless hardships after exerting the ability to set foot on grounds void of restrictions is exhilarating. No longer bound, shackled, or held against my will, I understood the apostle Paul when he emphatically declared that where the spirit of the Lord is, there is liberty! And it's sweet!

Chapter 3

By Faith 5:7

"For we walk by faith, not by sight."

It's hard attempting to navigate through this world without some sort of map, compass, or keen sense of direction. The vastness of the world can be intimidating when we are destined to arrive at a specific location and don't have the tools to get us where we need to be. Today's technology offers us many options but one that is most readily used is Global Positioning Systems--GPS--that allows satellites that have been positioned in space to track certain signals to precisely pinpoint where we are at any given moment with astronomical accuracy. As it is true physically, so spiritually it is. It is equally as difficult to maneuver anywhere in the Spirit realm without having the properly exercised guidance and direction of the Holy Spirit. One thing is for certain, without faith we can do nothing! And without faith, it is IMPOSSIBLE to please God!

As a child I was peculiar yet intelligent, mostly quiet and rather shy. Much to my surprise, this didn't prove to be an effectively winning combination for becoming gainfully popular among my peers. I found myself alone, being my own best friend and this caused an array of negative emotions to emerge that fed a deeply rooted, unresolved desire to always look to please others and *be* pleasing to others, oftentimes at a great cost. I can recall numerous occasions in school where I gave others my lunch or lunch money to prove that I could become self-sacrificing for their temporary approval. Each time it only left me starving, broken, and naively desiring validation from people who couldn't have cared less.

I aimed hard to be everybody's friend, whatever they needed at that point in their lives, I strove to be. At times I cared nothing about my own health or well-being. In the dead of winter I would offer my coats and sweaters to kids that had forgotten theirs or did not have one and foolishly forced myself to be without, placing my own health at risk. Maybe if others saw the lengths I would go to make them happy or the menial reasons I would consider becoming their sacrificial lamb, somehow they would in turn feel compelled to do the same for me.

Unfortunately, until this time I doubted that anyone would count me worthy of such acts of kindness. It's easy to see how children can get caught up in vying to become the class clown because I did this often by acting out of character when I had an audience. I starved for a laugh and temporary rush from the short-lived approval of others. Needing constant validation created a vicious, self-defeating cycle of hurt, disappointment, and depletion of self that would exist well into my young adult years.

Oftentimes as a child I wanted desperately to please God but not in a sensible or advantageous manner and would do so through countless acts of works that were empty. Ritualistically giving of myself by way of depleting myself of many treasured material goods, performing a series of kind acts or simply saying long, extravagant prayers were all good things to do under the right guise, but executing these conventions thinking that I was earning special brownie points with God proved to be completely illogical. I was extremely proud of myself for what I assumed were the things I was supposed to do in order to please God, but it would be years before I realized that these were all things *I* could perform in my *own* strength. None of it required God to *do* anything, to *be* anything for me or to *believe* that He could. I had no concept of faith being the substance of things hoped for and the evidence of things not seen. Everything that could be done or attained had to be directly in front of me, seen and tangible in most instances.

There were plenty of circumstances and instances throughout the course of my childhood that I could have believed

God for healing and deliverance. I could have believed that God could see and righteously deal with every one of my perpetrators of molestation and sexual abuse that inflicted fear, doubt, and worthlessness in my life. I could have believed God for the understanding of my mother's compromised mental condition and why she had to leave my brother and me to be raised by my father. I could have believed that my inner beauty far outshined my outer flaws just as the sun's rays radiate brighter in unclouded days than when it's dark and raining. I could have believed that God would still manifest His plan in and through me although I had become a pregnant, teenaged, daughter of a preacher. I could have believed all that He says about me in His Word instead of consistently trading it for what others felt, believed, or assumed about me.

The sad thing is I didn't. Life had to back me up into many corners and I had to periodically be thrown into the Lion's Den at the mercy of my enemies before I realized that my own strength was detrimentally limited, but it was at these same points when my spiritual muscles began to gradually emerge as soon as I traded my weaknesses for His strength.

When I had no one else to explain to or to make sense of what was quickly transpiring and unraveling in my life, and all avenues of help that I knew of or exhausted had long been depleted, there was no one else left standing but God! Only because of what He had promised me years prior did I began to trust His words and undoubtedly believe what He had so clearly spoken. It was then that I remembered one attribute of God: He cannot lie, so His Word is true *and* His Word concerning me is true. I had to learn that God is completely trustworthy! There is no shadow of turning in Him, meaning that where there appears to be a shadow, darkness is somewhere near. But the Word declares that God is light—light always eliminates darkness.

I can tell you about the darkness of being teenaged, unmarried, and pregnant, while being the daughter of a prominent community figure and Pastor; there were some days I felt I would never make it out of the breathtaking abyss alive. I was completely bound and trapped in physically, emotionally, and spiritually. Here I was carrying life but could hardly withstand managing my own. My wildest imaginations can only fathom the intense anxiety of Mary, the mother of Jesus, and the uncertainty about the future of her unborn son as well as her own. She was only a teenager, not fully aware of what opportunities the entire world had to offer and her support system was seemingly rather small.

The scrutiny this young girl had to endure and the silence of all the stares, even the pointing, condemning fingers and wags of heads outwardly displaying utter disapproval, did not leave much room for genuine love to be shown. Somehow, with encouragement from her immediate circle of confidants and a powerful host of angels to support her, as well as the great work that was being produced in her, she survived it!

Inferred in the Gospel of Matthew, when a fully-termed Virgin Mary had greatly travailed in labor and desired to have a place of rest to deliver the Son of God, was a scene of divine humbleness. How amazing it was to have such unpretentious beginnings! Who could fathom that anything good could come out of a place that appeared to be void of elaborate surroundings and perfectly-made circumstances? The question was asked in the Bible whether any good thing could come out of Nazareth anyway. The question I asked of myself now was, COULD ANYTHING GOOD COME OUT OF ME? As for Nazareth, yes, quite amazing things did come out of a place and from a person whom people never suspected it ever could or would! Could this also be applied to me? Yes, it has and, yes, it will! I've discovered that treasures and riches are normally hidden in the most unsuspecting places, but when found they are blessings to the seeker.

In the same way as Mary, I discovered that I had an angel assigned to me amongst the host of my own insignificant inner circle. In and through the witnessing of the works in her life, I learned about unwavering faith. That one angel was my grandmother, Louise, a true giver of God. Over the span of my childhood, even into my early adult years, the lessons embedded inside every crook, cranny, and crisis spoke louder than any words the world's greatest orator could have ever spoken, but my grandmother had a gift for speaking words full of life, love, and grace that impacted me and remained like no other.

Amazingly, it was her unsurpassed faith that consistently awed me! Sometimes I would think that Grandma would be praying and speaking the craziest things; nevertheless whatever she would pray and declare soon came to fruition. Being a witness to her numerous answered prayers caused me to become curious as to what this formula consisted of for God to mightily move on one's behalf. As I recalled the different events, situations, and circumstances of each encounter, they implored me to keep record of them in my mind, heart, and soul.

Grandma was a woman of menial means; she didn't accumulate great material possessions. A few things she had an abundance of were a fluent prayer life with God and the immense ability to be a giver. The more it seemed my grandmother lacked on the surface, such as living in substandard housing and having shortages of adequate cash flow, the more abundantly God allowed my grandmother to give! She was well known in her community and beyond for giving from a place of overflow, a place of plenty, and was well represented as an eternal reservoir to family, friends, and enemies alike.

Grandma's house was known to be a safe haven frequented by those who were cast down, downtrodden, lost, and abused. Most would come because they were called to drop in and pick up whatever she had portioned out for them that day, in addition to a comforting word of encouragement, laughter or prayer that she would often offer up. Just as quickly as Grandma would give, it would return some 30, some 60, and some 100-fold back into her life or the lives of those she'd been praying and interceding for.

It was amazing to be a firsthand witness of the Word of God literally coming off the pages of the Bible I read and transformed into real life where it speaks of giving and it shall come back to you, good measure, pressed down and shaken together shall men give into your bosom. Her unwavering faith that God would supply her every need according to His riches in glory was the epitome of the joyous walk she enjoyed daily with Jesus until the day of her death.

God had indeed showed Himself mighty in the life of my grandmother, as well as my own. There were days as a child that I remember running through her house and would find her quietly sitting on the side of her bed interceding and praying. Sometimes there would be tears streaming down her face and at other times she sat with an erect posture and hands folded. She would pray so long sometimes that I assumed she was asleep, until I would unknowingly interrupt her prayers only to hear, "Hush! I'm praying"! and I knew she meant business.

Day and night without fail she would pray and, yet more, God would answer. Literally, she did not see how ends were going to meet, but she always trusted in the God who had pulled her through being widowed with five young children and adopting two additional ones, seeing them all go to college and never see a prison or jail cell, and witness all of them work in ministry in different capacities. She knew God to be nothing short of faithful and a keeper over His Word. These were where the lessons of standing in faith, unwavering, were derived from, regardless of what circumstances presented themselves. These are the truths I absorbed from closely observing my Grandma Louise; in hard times, stand. In happy times, stand. Even when it seems the enemy has the upper hand, continue to stand being confident that the God who had begun a great work was able to complete it and He would effectively fight and defeat every battle.

What seemed like a meager existence of having nothing but God and His goodness to carry me through tough times, taught me much more about the importance of having and keeping a strong faith in God than I had recollected. Lessons of unconditional love and how God can turn little into much made me realize just how rich my grandma truly was. It caused me to understand just how much more wealthy the recipients of this unblemished love and effectual prayer were as well. Beyond this, I know for a surety that some situations would not have worked out as smoothly as they have if she hadn't already laid up prayers for her seeds that remained on the Earth.

So now faith is the substance of things hoped for and the evidence of things not seen and we walk by faith and not by sight. Learning to grow in faith was adapted by seeing faith being worked out in others. Although faith cannot within itself be seen, God sends representatives onto the earth to show His glory through and, in turn, their faith in Him becomes contagious to the faithless and can be seen indisputably by others. Living, breathing, walking epistles, their testimonies and trusting God through life's hardships are true elements of evolving faith. Without faith, we wither and waiver needlessly.

Chapter 4

Things Seen Are Temporal 4:18

"While we look not at the things which are seen, but at the things which are not seen: for the things which are seen *are* temporal; but the things which *are* not seen are eternal."

Oftentimes, we are mesmerized by elements of surprise; some are found just above the surface while yet other articles have to be searched out because they are hidden. We are spell-bound by mechanisms that carry a tempting level of mystery. It is this kind of mystery that excites and awakens our curiosity. There is something inviting about objects that are known to exist but cannot easily be seen; those things that seem almost invisible and virtually out of sight, yet keenly sensed enough to tantalize and tempt the mind.

It's just in our human nature to seek after, discover, and conquer this type of excitement for our own fleshly pleasures. Bright, beautiful packages laced with ribbons, bells, and bows. Sheer lace and transparent veils that vaguely expose the silhouette of an image that appears to be hidden close behind. Both fuel our hunger to know what's inside and behind them. At times, these are components found in the depths of vivid imaginations of man, which if given the opportunity and fueled with intent and time, lead to sin. Eventually, once sin has found a resting place, the final destination is death.

I cannot recall the first encounter that I had with "Death" but when she entered my life, it was apparent that she had already laid her stake to claim the peace and tranquility I had in my world and had become accustomed to at that time. Her sole purpose was to appear intimidating, larger than life and invincible. Death was smooth and, initially, undetectable. The reason she was able to operate at the outset incognito is because she came packaged with all the frills and thrills such as the career, the independence, and the intelligence that the highest bidding suitor could buy.

That bidding, blind suitor just happened to be my father—the one who was my world and simultaneously my heart and I believed these facts were indisputable. The plans that were put into play by Death were to use the oldest war tactic known to man—divide and conquer! If she would execute it effectively, then she would have to begin with the subject she felt would be subservient to her through weakness, and at the moment, I fit the bill.

I only appeared weak! Although I was embarrassingly shy and extremely quiet, I had a relationship with the Father that was fortified and strengthened when I communed often with Him through the Spirit. By this stage in my life, quite a few whirlwinds had blown into it and somehow while they were in the midst of violently raging, a great shaking occurred and unearthed my God-given voice. I lost it! Naturally when something valuable is lost, the initial reaction is fear. It is the kind of fear that whatever has been taken, stolen, and carried away will not be returned. Eventually, Death would be defied and rendered powerless.

It was a Saturday. As a child this was my favorite day of the week. I spent countless hours writing short stories, drawing, changing my doll's hairstyle, and creating new dishes in my Easy-Bake oven. Isolating myself and attempting to create moments of joy was what I did best, especially when Daddy wasn't around. It was Quarterly Meeting weekend where Friday night was set aside for the business of the church. Saturdays were an all-day event with the evening ending in Communion and Foot Washing.

Sundays were to fellowship with whichever church was scheduled to have Quarterly Meeting with us and we all enjoyed a big, delicious meal after services together. Our family resided in Raleigh, N.C., but we commuted to Greenville every Sunday for the church services. We did this for more than 10 years before moving to Greenville.

Daddy would go to Greenville by himself during the Quarterly Meeting weekends and then come to get us for the Sunday morning church services. Death was a nurse and had a different schedule and would be the "babysitter" for my brother and me simply because a relationship with Death until this time was nonexistent. We just didn't know her. By the time my father and Death were married, we had only met her twice. Between the summers that we spent with Grandma and the weekends at other relatives and friends houses, there weren't any blocks of time to get to know each other. It was absolutely devastating to be forced to call this unknown assailant "Mama." Nevertheless, with much reserve and regret, the request to do so was performed as requested.

I recall it being my second encounter alone with Death. Maybe the first encounter was used to scope me out, to study me in order to learn my strength and weaknesses, but the persistence of Death ultimately calculated the same techniques as Satan had with Eve when he caused Adam and her to fatally fall. Hidden away in my Saturday safe haven, I was suddenly interrupted and summoned by Death to complete another randomly commanded chore. Without hesitation and rendered in complete submission, the task had been completed. I turned away in anticipation of rushing back to my creative space only to be provoked by Death to come back and not move until inspection was satisfactorily conducted and until the follow-up command was given to resume normal duties.

I stood still, facing Death with a pleasant gaze on my face because I was pleased with the quality and completeness of what had been asked. Did I tarry in responding to her beckoning? Had I looked confused when the orders were yelled out? I could not understand why Death had this glare in her eyes, nor could I decipher where this evil, twisted grimace had erected. Death had turned into something unrecognizable in a matter of seconds, and for no apparent reason. As I stood frozen, scared, and confused, I felt a swift sting to the right side of my face! She had slapped me! Death had *slapped* me...Death had slapped *me*.

Heartbroken, shattered, disappointed, and utterly confused, I stood, trying to find the answer as to why in her eyes, but they were misleading due to the emptiness and darkness I observed in them. This was the ultimate betrayal! I thought I had returned to the place where I could allow another adult in my coveted space and believe they possessed some degree of good in them, the kind that children love to gravitate toward and not run away from. But this would not be the case with Death, not now, not ever.

As I held my pounding head, I sulked and cried my way back to my room. Still baffled over the recent occurrences, I rehearsed in my head how I would tell my dad about the story that made no sense. How could I "tell" on another adult? Adults always seemed to have a secret code of rules where children were not allowed to speak against them or say things that would adversely put the adults at odds with each other.

I wanted Daddy so badly to know how horrible of a choice he'd made in making Death his wife and my brother and my potential "Mom." I did not want to be responsible for any discord or fighting, not on my account. Naturally, I was the peacemaker and desired for everyone to get along, even if it killed me on the inside and placed my own piece of mind at stake. I wouldn't be the cause of someone else's unhappiness, especially not Daddy's. So I didn't tell. As a result, I sunk deeper into the deadly, quiet hole that I so desperately attempted to climb out of; a place that welcomed weak, deadened spirits and lost, silenced souls. For now, Death had gained the victory.

As I became older, the gap between my father and me widened. The more he believed the façade Death routinely performed, the more my brother and I lost footing in the only ally we had left to rescue us from this living hell. Year after year the ante was heightened. The Quarterly Meeting shenanigans persisted and Death's personality continued to turn intermittently like a light switch.

Sometimes I didn't believe Daddy's car had completely pulled out of the driveway before Death's alter ego morphed, took control, and held me hostage. Surprisingly, there were no more angry slaps to my face, just instances of crippling intimidation and gut-wrenching ridicule. Death would spew venom in such a calculated way that oftentimes it had me questioning whether my sanity was intact. She made fun of my quiet nature, my looks, and even my moments of timidity. Quite a bit of time would elapse before I would become enlightened that these are normal practices of bullies, because they hardly ever feel valuable themselves. Instead they consistently battle with the demons of inadequacy, shame, and guilt. Readily, bullies harass others to make themselves attain some sense of leverage and desire to appear superior to their victims.

Death played the game well. She had mastered the oldest tactic of war--divide and conquer. Daddy was conquered by her love and I was equally confined by her hate. Effectively, she found new ways to further separate and isolate me from the comfort and love of my father, or so it seemed. As I constantly fought for my life and contended for the value and cost of my oil, I soon recognized that not even the enemy could deny the Lord's hand and anointing on my life. Actually, this distinct fragrance was what had originally attracted Satan and his attacks to me in the first place.

I had entered a season of depression. And this was before I even understood what this ailment was or the circumstances in which it could exist. I began losing interest and focus in the things that I once loved. During this time in my life I had been concentrating on using my creativity in writing short stories and applying my gifts in diverse ways like through artistic drawings and sculpturing hair. I lost it all, and fast! The overwhelming emptiness felt as if I was departing on a long, dreaded field trip far away to a secluded, unknown location and somehow missed the bus to return home!

I was terrified, lost, and alone with no real help in sight. As a child subjected to this despondent state of mind, the ability to function normally was next to impossible. Every day before I would enter the house after school, a spirit of dread would come upon me as if to say, The party is over. Your temporary escape through the classrooms at school and the chaotic, yet peaceful bus ride home has abruptly come to an end. Reminder: This is Hell. Welcome back! Immediately, I remember having this sickening churn in the pit of my stomach, along with bouts of anxiety that ran rapidly through my chest because I did not know what this particular day, or any day for that matter, would hold. This daily experience could be likened to walking through an eerie, haunted house not knowing what could be lurking around the corners to attack you. Surely, the enemy had his grip on me!

The gradual distance and blinding fog between seeking the love and sensing the protection I once knew so well was becoming increasingly dense to the extent that I no longer discerned or recognized it. To my dismay, Love had moved far away and obtained another residence. In this moment I was an uninvited guest and the quest to regain Love would take many years.

I fought endlessly day after day for years, for the attention and love of my father. There were other contenders in the ring as well: his wife, his church and his community. The reigning title always appeared to go to his church. Any family time, which was extremely rare, had to be factored in around the never-ending events, meetings, conferences, or revivals the church calendar had.

That meant that the ability to take family vacations to catch up on everyone's updated progression in life was nonexistent, even though we all lived under the same roof. I couldn't understand how we were all so divided, yet seemingly suffered from the very same ailments—lack of love and attention. In reality, this should have knitted us closer together. Love, in this sense, equated to time and adequate attention.

Again, it was a Saturday. Only this Saturday was four years later. By now I was 16 and a teenaged mother of a 9-month-old that had not begun to walk yet. My baby was accustomed to taking her bath inside the hollow, deep-seated sink that was in the kitchen right off from my room downstairs. The scene is the same, with the main characters in place. Daddy had excused himself to a morning business meeting at the church again, which sparked Death's bitterness to be conjured up, again.

These instant replays of vile misbehavior and misdirected anger were played out a little too often for my liking and I had little to no tolerance for the reoccurring foolishness. Due to the familiar episodes and its predictable nature, I developed a hardened exterior and a rebellious resilience to the tactics of Death. I would no longer be the pun of her jokes, the target for her bouts of violence, and a sounding board for the moments she ranted and fired rounds of negative, spirit-crushing ammunition.

I had grown tired of my cries falling upon deaf ears. My voice had long been silenced because no one desired to attend to my gaping wounds, so I just bled, alone. With each drop of vivacity leaving my soul by the second, the harder I sought to contend for the life I knew could be possible. Recognizing this truth unmasked the beast that had been hidden inside of me that confirmed that I was worth fighting for. It was time to risk it all—this time would be different. Today was not the day, Devil!

"I said to take her upstairs and give her a bath in the family bathtub," she yelled angrily.

"But she's never taken a bath up there! Why does she need to start today," I defiantly responded, bracing myself for the inevitable.

"...because I said so!'

As Death charged toward me, she had intended for the slap she executed toward my face to make contact but a quick sidestep caused that to fail. For her impulsive action, my reaction soon followed and we ensued with several blows at one another until the last one was discovered to have made contact with her face and shattered her glasses. I laughed! I had resulted to provoking fury and displaying gestures of ridicule toward Death because at this moment I wanted her to feel every bit of hurt and shame she had thrust upon me over the years. I sought to humiliate her and uncover her weaknesses as she had done mine through exerting domination over every situation.

As she stood there with the twisted pair of glasses now hanging from one side of her face, I felt relief! This was not how things were supposed to play out, especially between a parent and a child, but something stood up in me and it made me feel empowered and strong, like I had been vindicated. I didn't have to endure any longer through harshness or be a victim of the psychological games or become the helpless punching bag, the scapegoat, or the sacrificial lamb begging for mercy at the hand of their enemy. For the moment, I was free and freedom felt good.

Suddenly I noticed that I was visibly trembling after recalling the recent act of violence. I had gone beyond the point of no return and I stood not knowing what to do or what was to come. Soon Death moved toward the phone that was stationed on the kitchen wall. She quickly picked it up and began dialing the police. With fists and teeth still clenched, I stood still and just listened to the conversation taking place over the phone.

"Yes, I need an officer at my house…my daughter just jumped on me!"

I gasped in disbelief! Did she just say that? She just told the authorities a boldfaced lie! I had reasoned within myself that if she could invent a story that quickly on her feet, who knows what she could be capable of given a little time and space. Springing into action, I only thought of my baby and what the police would do when they arrived.

Not too long after the call, an officer arrived. As soon as he came into the house, she rushed in to explain the occurrences, only the tale was one-sided. I was not given the opportunity to say much of anything before Death screamed, "I want her out of my house! Her and her baby, I want both of them out of my house!"

And without too much hesitation the officer explained, "Well, Ma'am, you and the baby are going to have to leave now. She's the owner of this house and she has the right to tell you to leave if she wants."

"But this is my daddy's house, too! I was just defending myself!"

"I'm sorry, Ma'am, but you're going to have to go."

Tears started to come, because I knew I had nowhere to go. As I dressed my baby, it became harder and harder not to hate Death. She actually detested me so much that she gave no thought to the well-being of my child. Now we were both out on our luck, with no place to go. About the time I had gathered a couple of things and headed out the door toward the porch, Daddy pulled up in the yard. Alas! Here was my ram in the bush!

"What's going on?! Y'all got the police all up at the house! What is the problem?"

His words were like sharp knives piercing me and slicing into my soul. My emotions couldn't withstand the embarrassment and immense disappointment he expressed on his face and I was shaken all over again. I figured I'd better take this opportunity to revisit all that had gone down before he went into the house to hear the perfectly twisted tale from Death. After he had his fill of the situation, he entered the house to inform the officer that he had it all taken care of. Death rolled her eyes and began to protest. She was furious to see that I had not gone anywhere and was allowed to stand inside her house again. My father who did not condone drama simply refrained from delving too deep into the details, waved his hands, and replied, "We'll discuss it later. No one is leaving."

For the first time in a long while, I felt safe and covered. For the first time in a long while, I felt coveted, like I was worth fighting for. Daddy showed me that he had the ability to stand for what was right where his granddaughter and I were concerned and this fact alone was exhilarating to me.

It's amazing how years of baggage can be released in just a moment. All it took was a single moment of grace to erase every foul action and deed that had been prepared against me to cause me to fail and fall prey to the enemy's devices. God is likened to this in that He allows so much to go on in our lives and at times it feels as if we will buckle and break under the pressures of it all, but then He steps in and just like a refreshing wind His grace and His power appears and fights for us!

Truth be told, we are all guilty at times of carrying too much baggage and weight when God has earnestly prodded us to release it all into His hands. His hands are mightier than ours, His patience is long, and His power is unmatched! When we are tempted to be the General, Commander-in-Chief or play Lone Ranger and navigate alone the war that has been waged against us, we decline the Lord's flawless record of wins, for the Word reminds us that each battle is not ours, but the Lord's.

The things that are seen are temporal and temporary, even those things that seem unmovable and constant such as the people, principalities, worries, stresses, and pitfalls of our lives, but one thing can be declared with a surety—trouble doesn't last always! These "Egyptians" (anyone or anything that had the ability to keep you bound and render you powerless) that you have seen before you (provoking you, taunting you, causing you to compromise and consider turning back) you shall see no more, forever. Forever!

Even our adversary, the devil, has an expiration date and his days of roaming the Earth to and fro will come to naught. Soon his tricks, deceits, and devices shall perish and become of no effect. Simply BELIEVE IT, STAND ON IT, and DECLARE IT!

Chapter 5

The Promises of God 1:20

"For all the promises of God in him *are* yea, and in him Amen, unto the glory of God by us."

Butterflies have always intrigued me purely because in nature they are teachers. From the beginning, the journey they are destined to embark on demonstrates how each of us should continuously be transforming and transitioning from one level of growth to the next. Destiny is multi-layered—wherever we are, a facet of destiny is. Whether we choose to follow our own way or the one that God provides, everyone has followed a destiny. Every decision, every place of question, all acts and deeds done are effectively being used to showcase where it is we are headed.

Often, I love to observe butterflies gracefully fluttering in mid-Spring, amidst the newly-bloomed array of flowers and strongly erected trees. The discreetness of their flight is amazing in that it reminds me of the countless, quiet whispers of God that continually express scores of hidden truths; if you're not vigilant and alert, you will miss it.

The Creator audibly and silently speaks repeatedly through creation, and butterflies are just one specimen of many that He uses. Every time I encounter one, instantly my spirit is overwhelmed with immediate expectation! Either God has chosen to use these opportunities to confirm the arrival of a promise or He is revealing new facets of Himself to me. Thus, butterflies represent a changing of tides and a resurrection of brand-new merciful beginnings. Butterflies also embody perseverance, longsuffering and patience; all of which are prerequisites in obtaining God's manifold blessings.

The butterfly's splendor is uniquely crafted--quite often imitated, but rarely duplicated and if you study them, timeless life lessons are found in who they are and what they become. Their multiple characteristics communicate volumes about the processes of growth and the evolution of authentic beauty. Resoundingly, the unspoken message of butterflies declares that although circumstances may have previously been ugly and unseemly, even to the extent of rendering its purpose and appearance unrecognizable at times, after enduring the process and being transformed through metamorphosis, a beautiful product is promised to emerge!

It is imperative to complete the process! Everything, in essence, is necessary. If the butterfly was ever unable to endure its process then its magnificence and its ability to effectively be seen as the evidence of God's grace while going *through* the process would never be revealed.

My father expressed this journey best when he declared these words (from the sermon "Holding On To Playthings" by Bishop Randy B. Royal):

"I was thinking about how beautiful butterflies are, but that all butterflies started out as worms. Butterflies were not always beautiful, but they were ugly, little squirmy things, crawling on the ground...but there was a butterfly mentality in their nature. And they refused to *remain* a worm because in their destiny was a butterfly. No matter what else they might have wanted to become, when the maturation began or when they matured, they became a beautiful butterfly and refused to stay where they were (evolution)."

The worm stage began very early in life for me. As a matter of fact, the effects from this ugly, grotesque, and prolonged phase have extended over into more than half of my adult life. When you are consistently inundated with the worm's mentality and mundane way of living, not much hope is found beyond your lowly dwelling of the ground. All there seems to be is what is right in front of you or within your surroundings and reach. Although I hadn't graced the Earth for a significant amount of time, it didn't take long for me to grasp the reality that I was truly living the life of a worm!

By the time I was 4 years old, I'd experienced the warm, loving embraces of both parents and the joys of them being young, married, and happy. I recall our family travailing through tough times and not always having the luxuries that other neighbors seemed to have, such as a reliable car. Daddy would take the bus or public transportation to work and the irony behind this truth is that he held a nice office position for the Department of Transportation. He would walk a half mile to the bus stop every morning and back home in the afternoons. When he would come in the door, Mom--who had been cooking--and I would wait in the kitchen until he ran over to give us a hug. Mom would get the longest hugs and I would break in between them and get the love from the middle.

This routine would go on day after day and week after week for some time, until the day it no longer did. Soon Daddy would come home to no food being cooked and heated arguments that lasted past dinner that he had to cook. I didn't like for them to argue, so I always burst out crying because the episodes would be so intense that they literally scared me. During these times I had a prized possession that I would run to for comfort and solace. Not recognizing the subjects of the loud battles between them, I spotted my inkling of peace on the countertop in the shape of a honey pot--it was my favorite thing, the cookie jar! In it were all kinds of treats, but none that I could ever overindulge in. It was safe, it never yelled or became angry or had me worrying about what it would do next. I loved it and my feuding parents knew it.

Unfortunately, in the course of one of these occurrences, my mother, whose temper could not be extinguished, grabbed the cookie jar and hurled it at my dad and it fell to the floor and was shattered into many unrecognizable pieces! At this moment, the aftermath mirrored the present condition of my heart. Who could mend it? Stunned, I could no longer cry but began shouting, "Stop! Stop!" hoping the rage my mother was displaying wouldn't be strong enough to kill both my dad and me. I was traumatized to my core because I felt targeted and defenseless. Furthermore, I was petrified about what might happen next. The fight had subsided for the night but would continue the next day. The vendetta would begin becoming more personal and a lot more destructive.

I needed to find another outlet; something that I could escape to and experience a euphoric state of safety. As far back as I could remember music had always been my saving grace. Much like the results from the music the young, shepherd boy David played in the Bible where he used the harp to effectively tame the savage beasts of Saul. Music had a medicinal, healing effect on me especially when I would encounter moments of despair; music was able to calm me in times of uncertainty. Both of my parents were exceptionally musically-inclined and each had played several instruments. Both were vocally astute as well.

Daddy had purchased my first kid-sized organ, the kind that plugged up in the wall, complete with a bench to sit on. Although I had not learned a chord or a scale, that organ meant the world to me! While most children my age were playing with blocks and dolls, I indulged in plinking the keys of my organ every chance I got, especially since the episodes of fussing between Mom and Dad were increasing and getting more intense. Somehow I found an escape from my anxieties through many unmatched, seemingly chaotic melodies I managed to arrange during these times.

One evening after returning home with Daddy, I noticed that my mother was not there. There was no lingering aroma of freshly cooked food or any glowing lights from the stove that would indicate something was baking inside. I ran to every room in the house hoping to find her in the bathroom or in their bedroom taking a nap. She was nowhere to be found. The pursuit of finding my mother was so intense that I had not recognized that my organ was now gone! All at once, the wall that the organ sat against was bare, naked, and bleak. Instantly, my heart acknowledged this familiar state of brokenness and knew the remedy would not come as readily as I had hoped. Shockingly, the whereabouts of the organ seemed to bother my father as well as he tried consoling me while holding his own lowered head inside the palm of his hand. I searched his eyes for answers to questions that this time surprisingly he did not have.

We moved out of the house and into a small, one bedroom apartment---just Daddy, my brother, and me. Things were peaceful, yet a bit uneasy at times due to the immediate relocation and the circumstances from which it all transpired. My parents were separated, but it wasn't long before my mother made her grand reappearance. Maybe Daddy wanted to explore the possibilities of the two of them rekindling the reason they had married in the first place. The ink was still wet on the marriage license since, by this time, only four years had expired. So the routine began. Fussing. Fighting. Chaos. Repeat. Soon, crates of glass bottles that Daddy saved in the kitchen after drinking his favorite sodas went crashing to the cemented floor. One bottle smashed after the other, until they were all gone.

My brother and I were so terrified that I grabbed his hand and we ran to the bedroom, crying, covering our ears, and closing our eyes. Somehow the turmoil still found a way to creep in and wreak havoc in our small minds. We decided to hold onto each other, sobbing in the dark, because if light had uncovered us it would illuminate the path for evil and unrest to find us. The next morning when Daddy was taking us to day care, Mama was not there. As he was attempting to whisk us quickly out of the door, I noticed that the floor-model TV had a huge hole, equal to the size of the screen in it. The only thing that remained was jagged pieces of glass around the perimeter of the set. Astonished, my brother and I pointed at the sight of the mass catastrophe and wept, as we both scooted by. Again, Daddy's eyes offered no answers.

When the divorce between my parents was final, my brother and I were awarded to our father. A few family members testified in the proceedings to state that my father was better suited to care for us. Apparently, my mother suffered from mental illness that prevented her from providing safety and care for us long term. In retrospect, being raised by Daddy turned out to be the better choice overall, but it would not be the easiest.

Daddy had been a Pastor since the beginning of my existence. There was always a program, an Assembly class or some other event that he and my family were made to be loyal to. It seemed as though every weekend was completely packed with tiresome formalities that all pertained to ministry that my brother and I could not effectively boycott at any time. His schedules were becoming tight and the churches in which he served were becoming more demanding. Daddy realized the challenges of keeping up with what the people needed of him. His ability to comply with his ministry's calls was mindboggling, especially with having no wife but being fully equipped with children caused him to make some ill-fated decisions. Soon my brother and I would be bounced around from stranger to stranger and from babysitter to babysitter over the next six years. Some faces we knew and others we did not. This marked the beginning of the end of normalcy, on many levels, in my life.

The next couple of years and the traumas that they bore would become very difficult for me to overcome. Some childhood scars can readily be doctored up, attended to, mended, and healed while others can take a lifetime to confront and conquer. My personality was one of shyness, insecurity and the need to make everyone happy, even if that meant to my own detriment. While there were various tangible possessions and people that had been removed from my life whether willingly or forcefully, I wanted to retain the power to keep those things within my immediate reach that brought me comfort or a sense of belonging. I never wanted to make anyone mad or they become displeased with my actions or behavior, so I would go above and beyond to make others like me. I behaved as close to an angel as I possibly could and although painful to do so, gave up personal, prized possessions just to receive a smile, a kind word, or some show of affection.

I was 6 years old when people began writing vile, unspeakable articles on my conscious, subconscious, and unconscious chalkboard. Sadly, the various forms of penmanship were all recognizable and dreadfully familiar to me. The fact that I appeared to need attention misled others to become comfortable with abusing me sexually. Being dropped off consistently from house to house among strangers every weekend did not help matters, but not all the perpetrators were strangers.

In fact, they were neighbors, friends of the family, and relatives; those I should have felt most relaxed and comfortable around. Maybe this is why the violators slyly remained unsuspecting because of the relationship that was already built with my father and other family members. Soon hands and other extremities ran down into my underwear constantly and fingers began to penetrate my most precious private areas. My underdeveloped breasts were fondled and sexual acts were being requested. Regardless of relentless, frightened protests, unwanted kisses, and role plays became a normal occurrence coupled with threats of promised harm if silence about these vile actions were ever voiced. With each episode I felt I was becoming further and further buried underground, with no chance of being rescued or sought after.

To present, I believe I was "studied" long before a violation was ever committed. Many that knew me knew that I was shy and would hardly speak to anyone and if the possibility arose, I needed excessive prodding before holding conversations. As a result, this made me an easy target, one not likely to tell of the frequent occurrences of abuse to adults nor one to be accused of revealing incriminating "secrets" against anyone.

In all actuality, the repeated, forced episodes caused my inner voice of self-advocacy against these evil, senseless acts to be shut completely down and utterly silenced! With each indiscretion, the fight within me died a slow, agonizing death. My spirit was crushed and my inability to recover from the last blow to my heart found no retreat. I needed God! I needed protection! I needed peace! UNHEARD, UNHEALED, and UNRULY; this would be the passageway for most of my tumultuous teen years, occurring at a time when others in this stage were trying to find themselves and claim their place in this world. Unfortunately, because I did not reveal these dark secrets until my early adult years, I had the task of traveling this problematic quest alone. Confusion mingled with mental warfare, accented by the nagging question of whether I was worthy of being loved by anyone or meant anything to anybody was a perfect discombobulation of lies and half-truths that the enemy would force-feed me regularly to render my future of serene freedom bleak.

Who could love and appreciate a worm anyway *except* a predator? Some people won't appreciate you until you've reached your end stages of destiny. Many have dealt with you on previous levels of the processes of your life for various reasons while you were yet being perfected but somehow along the journey they chose not to go the whole way with you. Their loss! Now in retrospect, they wished they hadn't so quickly dismissed you in your cocoon season. Fact is most of them that started out with you in your worm stage won't be there to witness the moment you quickly shed the dead weight of the things that kept you encased from your true form of destiny; neither will they catch sight of you suddenly emerging into the greatness purposed *for* you unless they were able to endure the maturation process *with* you. As a butterfly with new eyes (vision) and newly attached wings (apparatus to move forward), oftentimes you will find that there remains no vacancy for them in your new life.

Considering the perceived afterthoughts of a newly-formed butterfly, who knew that before I could comprehend the Promises of God that I was already the recipient of them! What He brings me to concerning my destiny is what was already in me. Destiny is discovering the hidden treasures that God has preordained for each of us inside this earthen vessel. When we are aligned and spiritually in tune with Him and trust His leading, we will no doubt be brought into good success.

Only God knew our ending before our existence! In trusting Him in my child-like fashion, I was able to hang onto hope. One of my favorite passages of Scripture lies in Jeremiah 29:11. The insight gained from this truth is that in life we must have two components to obtain any promise. First, you must have a *HOPE* of something and secondly, a *FUTURE* in which to obtain it. Honestly, we cannot have one without the other, for your hope is in something that isn't presently seen today but is believed to be coming soon. Without laying hold on the sights of HOPE, we will never be equipped to entertain the possibility of a FUTURE. Hope deferred realizes that something of significance was lost and the strength needed to regain it becomes void; thus, the FUTURE of the thing hoped for is nonexistent. Therefore, both of these vital elements of claiming any promise must work simultaneously. Finally, what a blessing it is to declare the very words of God Himself where All the Promises *in Him* are YEA (yes) and AMEN (it is so!); outside of Him there is no unquestionable HOPE and no tangible FUTURE.

Just as the butterfly was among the shattered and unrecognizable pieces of his cocoon, in and through me with hope, God was able to fashion a unique masterpiece; an exclusive work of Heavenly art.

Chapter 6

Lest Satan Should Get an Advantage 2:10-11

"When you forgive this man, I forgive him, too. And when I forgive whatever needs to be forgiven, I do so with Christ's authority for your benefit, so that Satan would not get an advantage of us: for we are not ignorant of his devices."

 Have you ever been to the doctor with ailments invading your body that you knew required some major attention, and fast? Imagine falling backward down a flight of stairs, losing consciousness for a short span of time, and finding yourself unable to move your limbs. Or think back to a time in your early parenthood years when you became irate as an overly concerned parent, and noticed that the nature of your baby's fever alarmed you. It had consistently remained too high for conventional medicines to touch, and by instinct you knew the hospital was the only other option available at that time of night?

 These scenarios given could vary in its severity on many levels, and so could the responses to them, but the line of reasoning suggest that emergency situations call for emergency solutions. Neither of these things could easily be ignored, but the pain and anguish from them would propel anyone to spring into action and wholly believe in an appropriate and timely resolution. Due to innumerable physical infirmities present today and their complexities, specialized care is provided to appropriately address a wide spectrum of conditions while qualified professionals are sought out to study their origins and determine the best plan of care. But what happens when it seems there is no help?

 People have always believed this widely accepted myth that the Preacher's Kids (PKs) were the worst behaved individuals and the worst character of people to walk the face of the Earth. What is amazing about this thought is that although it may appear to have some relevance or element of truth, we're oftentimes the most mistreated and misunderstood! When a parent or an individual has been called to the Ministry of God, the people whom they lead esteem their leader to a certain level of astute godliness, which is both delusional and senseless. Sadly, there exist a set of unspoken, unattainable criteria as to how to maintain such godlike qualities although the composition of such qualities remains unknown. Throughout much of life, I have witnessed that people often bear the need to obtain an attachment to *someone* or *something* bigger than themselves and here in the earthly realm, Pastors and those individuals who serve in ministry are regarded as being next to God.

Furthermore, the children of these Pastors and how they are commonly beheld by the council, better known as the public, are a horse of a different color altogether! With the faultiness of these skewed perceptions, there seems to be neither refuge nor relief for Pastors or their vulnerable offspring, except in God.

Growing up in the Church, I spent countless years witnessing various impaled individuals, both spiritually and physically, that had become disabled by situations or circumstances sent to destroy them. Their initial response to their assorted conditions was to come to the church, hear the Word of God, ask His forgiveness, seek after and surrender to God with reckless abandonment and, in turn, immediately be forgiven and healed. And I know for a fact that they received from God what they had asked and sought after because the evidence followed them; whether through their affirming transformation in appearance, change in behavior, or increased belief and faith in God. All of these represented steadfast evidence in God's miraculous power to transform anyone found in any condition. There was no question in my mind about the existence of God and no one could convince me that He was not real or that He never took care of His own. Until now, He had taken care of everything concerning me, both destructive and beneficial in nature.

I was 15 and just as the seasons change from year to year, so did the seasons in my life. Everything had finally settled to a manageable medium, not that things were perfect but there was a notable hiatus in- between the vast valleys. Where there was once the joy and contentment of the season of Spring approaching, the brisk, bitter winds of Winter had abruptly returned and settled in, because now I was pregnant.

Finding myself completely lost in love with a boyfriend I believed epitomized the meaning of true love and fantasizing about the potential of a love-filled life only due to carrying his unborn child, I never thought for one minute that my life was over. Yes, I'd made very poor choices that resulted in my untimely, unplanned pregnancy. Nevertheless, no one had ever informed me about the unspoken clause in the Bible, the one that states if a female becomes pregnant out of wedlock, their destinies were forever tied up in the pits of Hell.

In addition to this, the most damaging clause of all was not vastly spoken but rather thought that because people can "see" your sin with their natural eyes is the same reason why your "sin" is ever before you, which suggests that there is no need to seek redemption, or have the desire to be made completely whole and be forgiven. See, people are under a mass, crippling deception that God operates like them. Even if some proclaim to have "the mind of Christ," their actions display an exponentially different version of His mind. Christ's mind consisted of loving the unlovable, forgiving the unforgivable, and considering others before ourselves. In contrast, the framework of our minds often is to condemn the condemnable, banish those that are lost, and place our opinions and judgments on others mercilessly.

There's something about being able to "see" the sin. Forget that some people struggle with gambling, indulging in pornography, abusing their spouses and children, cheating on their taxes, and lying to their Pastors *and* God. We become frenzied about the seen things and readily excuse those "private" matters, especially if our actions are found among them. If only those darkened walls that we hide behind and thrust our imperfections upon could talk. The stories they'd disclose would reveal elements scarcely found in the best horror stories. Unassumingly, we're compelled to solicit ourselves to darkness' devices, assuming the activities acquired within will remain there, but the Bible says to be sure that your sins will find you out. Eventually, truth shines its light upon the face of darkness, whatever type it is.

Such is found in the example where condemnation meets transformation, through an initial sermon of an unlikely candidate. The parallel between my life and hers, and the mask of the struggle she battled with internally, is unreal! In John 4:1-42, the Bible tells a narrative between Jesus the Savior and the woman at the well, a well-known sinner. Before this exchange ever took place there were obstacles set up in the societal culture of that day that would have annihilated the possibility of the mass revival that soon would take place.

First, Jesus being a Jew understood that Jews and Samaritans were to have no dealings with one another. Samaritans were considered the half-breed cousins of Jews and had second-class status without question in their society. Secondly, this woman went against the rule of her customs that only allowed the women to fetch water at evening, when the other women were permitted to draw. Lastly, this woman's reputation preceded her because she was tangled up in an illicit relationship with a man who was not her husband, therefore willfully existing in a sinful lifestyle of adultery.

Everyone knew this woman's little secret; she had been married five times and now was found to have a live-in boyfriend. No one bothered to delve into *why* this woman experienced so many dead-end relationships that left her more and more depleted physically, mentally, and spiritually. The Bible didn't tell of anyone who had conducted a social history to determine the predispositions of the potentially deadly detours this woman had taken to propel her to this demise. No one! The community only concerned themselves with what they could see. They *saw* different husbands come and go. They *saw* how she was unable to be fulfilled by their companionship and acts of love. They *saw* how quickly she replaced men to fill voids in her life and how if any children were produced in these marriages, they were confused about whom to call Daddy. Nevertheless, this next encounter with a man would not end as the rest had, for what He would deposit in her would become permanent and, thankfully, her saving grace as well as a testament for those of us who find similarities parallel to hers!

Although this unnamed woman was kept under a spectating eye and the people around her fine-toothed the details of her life, her audience would soon stand at attention to receive this new-found evangelist and the life-changing message she carried. Jesus, who knew every aspect of this woman's life, did not choose to publicize it in the streets nor drag her before a condemning council, but dealt with her and the sin one-on-one. She had already been bashed, embarrassed, and ridiculed by those closest to her and by the ones she knew so well.

In order to be received by this broken vessel, Jesus needed to execute the polar opposite of what everyone else's tactics were in dealing with this woman. Rather, He had shown her more love than the husbands and the fair-weather friends she had dealt with before. They all were unable to get to the depths of the issues and were not spiritually equipped to deal with the *"why"* by focusing so needlessly on the *"what,"* but through the Word of God spoken through Jesus, He supplied the cure!

She was a sinner just like each of us, but her spirit lacked the wholeness it desperately sought after through materials and man. Satan knew that experiencing lack of love was our stronghold. If only we had received the amount of love that we felt we needed, the abundance and overflow of love that fostered indestructible exteriors in individuals, where no harm from the hands of others or danger from the mouths of others would be able to penetrate. Yet, undoubtedly, I connect to this unnamed woman because she went through a series of men in a quest for what they could not effectively give her--love.

I was this woman at the well, young, naïve, and fallen. Instead of encountering Jesus at the well, I had known Him through prayer and having a relationship with Him during my childhood. I often felt His presence in His house, the church, but when I needed refreshing in a very dry time in my life, the people with the condemning mouths, condemning eyes, and condemning behaviors, stood between me and the only way to my deliverance.

We do crazy things for love and the need to be loved and the Pastor's daughter was no different. I, too, sought love in all the wrong places. Consistently hearing about the love of God being preached by my father to many congregations and not being able to feel it, other than through monetary and other tangible means, it became more difficult to believe that God still had a plan for my life or that I was still worthy of His calling. As strong and invincible as I thought my dad to be, I expected him to do something that he could not do; shield me from the effects and depths of hurt I would be subjected to from the people he coveted and loved—his church.

Church folk taunted me and fervently pushed for me to abort the child I was carrying because eventually walking around in the state I was in was sure to bring shame to my father and, more so, on the ministry. It was done as if to imply that because I made poor choices, due to several incidences of unaddressed sexual abuse and several other buried issues in childhood, they would somehow rub off and eliminate the calling and election from God on his life or mine for that matter.

To make matters worse, if I thought the Mothers or Elders of the church would cover and pray for me or plead mercy on my pitiful behalf, I was dead wrong! As a matter of fact, I could not be acknowledged or spoken to because I was excommunicated. Not knowing what this meant, I asked my father to explain. He made clear that this was a term the church used when a person had committed a sin that banned and separated them from the church until the individual came back, stood before the church, and openly repented of the sin. Baffled and broken, I sadly pondered the words just spoken and wondered, "Had I sinned against *God* or the *church*?"

My mind went back a few months prior to another young, teenaged girl who actively sang in the choir that became pregnant out of wedlock and she was not made to endure this same undue treatment as I did. It was at this point that I understood that I was being made a spectacle, even an example of *because* I was the Pastor's daughter and realized that most of these actions were initiated to appease the people of the church and not bring about true restoration. I soon began to wonder if God played favorites, too.

Persecuted, condemned, and exiled, combined with feelings of abandonment, I felt there was nowhere to run, hide, or turn. With each passing day, I felt more and more disconnected from God and His people. How could these people be so cruel and heartless amidst my true hour of need? These Holy Ghost-filled, tongue-talking, Bible-toting, saved folks tried hard to kill my spirit before it even had a chance to live.

In like manner, King Herod had hunted for Jesus because He was the child of promise who would come and not only change but save the world. Operating within a contrary rationale, I was only a child thrust into an adult situation and needed much guidance but, even more than that, I needed to be heard, loved, understood, and covered by this ever-loving Savior! I was still held captive and hadn't been healed from previous transgressions against me that occurred beyond my control. However, the accumulation of past wounds and reoccurring, unresolved matters left me with the fruition of what potentially can happen when issues are left ignored and unattended.

Dejected in spirit and battling emotionally as though I had cast my pearls before trampling swine, my grandmother was the constant, positive force that remained true to who she was and her God-given gift of unbiased love ushered peace during turbulent times. Specifically throughout this time, when no one else's voice was heard, my grandmother made hers distinctively known. I recall the first time I sat in front of her being full with child and remembered feeling as though I had disappointed her or let her down. My emotions wouldn't allow me to speak, my ears went deaf, and my eyes were heavy with shame. What happened next was extremely surprising but healing! She spoke softly to ask how I was doing and with the look of grace on her face, she reassured me that she loved me. It was as if she was extracting all the hurt, pain, confusion, and anxiety I had stored inside of me for so long. She never condemned me, she never gave a cross or condescending word, but she applied grace and consistently offered her love *and* her support. If it had not been for this specific display of unfailing, unconditional love, I can guarantee that I would not have survived!

Isn't it amazing how when you think God has forgotten about your case He ushers in the most unsuspecting advocates to conceal and cover your cause when you can't speak for yourself? Indeed, I had been persecuted, but when I look back and think things over, I was never forsaken. God had shown me again that He was an ever-present help in times of surmounting trouble.

From the timeless poem "Invictus" this portion speaks directly *to* and *about* me: "My head was bloodied, but unbowed." Yes, I had taken quite a few licks but His grace cushioned every deadly blow. God kept me! He did not forsake me.

If I had to be made an example, then so be it! As Jesus declared in His Word, no man takes my life but I lay it down of my own accord, for I have been given the authority to lay it down and the authority to pick it up again. Satan thought he gave occasion to take advantage of what seemed like a bleak situation, but God has taken this same situation and turned it around for my good. Now, like the nameless woman at the well, I am declaring to others who have been dismissed, rejected, and cast out that all hope lies in the crucial encounter of you meeting Jesus, for He indeed holds the answer to all of this life's problems, issues, and mishaps. As the woman at the well learned, when you have received this drink, you shall thirst no more! Take the plunge! Refreshment is found by all who draw there.

Chapter 7

Perfect in Weakness 12:9

"And he said unto me, My grace is sufficient for thee: for my strength is made perfect in weakness. Most gladly therefore will I rather glory in my infirmities, that the power of Christ may rest upon me."

By this time in my life, I had celebrated a few significant successes that included earning three degrees; one in Cosmetology, one in Human Services and one in Life. Things were extremely difficult seeing as I was trying to maintain a job, raise two girls, and go back to school to complete an undergraduate degree in Social Work. This had been a lifelong dream of mine since I was young. My father often expressed how he wanted me to become a lawyer, something I believed he longed to achieve himself. However, I often had dreams and visions of helping the underprivileged and the disadvantaged, preferably those that were homeless. With the limitless imagination I possessed, I believed that anything that I conceived as far as helping others was definitely possible. Somehow the trials that I was experiencing weren't fierce enough to kill my drive at attaining a better life, not only for myself, but for my children and family as well, and getting it done by any means necessary!

Throughout my life God had executed a unique way of communicating *to* me and *through* me. As He had used my grandmother on countless occasions through her distinctively prophetic dreams she would have about people and death, He decided to use me in this very same way, instead with a specific, visible sign--a cloud. Whenever my grandmother would have a dream about someone dying, at times, she would share all that God had revealed to her. Indeed, each time she had these visitations of

God, they occurred with accuracy. I realized early that she possessed a gift and she coveted it as such; it was no plaything. I was in my early adult years when I discovered that I, too, had this gift.

My first experience with the gift appeared one Sunday after church. There was an older woman who was a member of the church that my family was fond of. She was the picture of health, no tell-tale signs of any illnesses or depravity. After each church service it was our custom to go around and greet everyone with either a hug or a handshake, as we said our "God bless yous" and our "See you laters." It was normal for our paths to cross each week and our encounters were normally concluded with a short sentence or two about random things.

This particular Sunday when I managed to get close to her, I witnessed a transparent cloud covering her face. She smiled and joked with others that were around her while I remained motionless and mute. *I saw the cloud*! I immediately asked God what this meant and if I should tell her what I was observing. He did not permit me to speak or to move, but to know in my spirit that a transition was about to take place. I wanted so badly to disclose to her what I saw but did not receive clearance to do so. The cloud followed her and remained covering her face until she left the premises. All I could do was pray. God had shown me this to prepare me for what would happen next. Early the next morning, my dad informed me that this woman had passed away and had died suddenly from a heart attack. No doubt I was bothered and heartbroken because of the closeness we had with one another; nevertheless, indeed God had prepared me for this. If I had received the news any other way, without preparation, I would not have been able to handle it.

As I pondered the sequence of events, I recognized that the transition took place in less than 24 hours, and I began to believe that God had allowed this gift to be used just this once, but I would soon discover that I was so wrong. The next appearance of the cloud would move closer to me than I wanted or thought.

Being a full-time student pursuing an associate's degree, I also held down a part-time job as a child-care assistant. It was here that I met two of my most treasured lifetime friends, one of whom was attending the same school as I but in a different field, and the other dedicated her life to impacting and enriching children's lives in unique ways. Significant memories were created that ultimately helped me to get through some crucial moments in my newly-saved life. I had not anticipated that the worst of these times would transpire here as well. There were weighty events to occur that tested my faith plus the longevity of my strength. Test and trials are necessary for the purposes of bringing forth and displaying God's grace upon us while enduring our valley experiences.

Fairly new to the faith, I purposely surrounded myself with individuals who openly served God and expressed His goodness daily. Finding a job that encompassed all of these attributes and more was truly a treasure. Inside the day care, the employees, and children awaited and enjoyed the daily devotions where we would gather together in a circle of unity and experience God through uplifting music, Scripture, prayer, and praise. It was during these intimate encounters with God that my personal walk with Him grew. Learning of Him and His ways quickly began to pay off in more ways than one. When faith is new, excitement is overflowing and as a result you feel like you can ask anything and it will materialize. Nothing seemed out of reach or off limits, and this place in God taught me exactly what I would need to endure the shadows of death that would come.

Teonti (Ms. Gillette), as she was affectionately called, was truly a godsend and on direct assignment from God to appear in my life at the moment she did. She, too, was a young adult that had grown up in the church and received Christ at an early age. She was trying to navigate through her adult years as a single, Christian woman, and without fail relied heavily on her faith. Although I had been subjected to numerous readings of the Bible from an early age, Teonti was able to help me comprehend Scripture in a new and profound way. We'd talk every day at work and every night for hours at a time about what we had learned new in the Word, how we were beginning to incorporate what we learned into the way we lived, and we'd often compare future plans that we prayed for and wanted God to answer. This was the highlight of most of my days as a new convert.

Right away Teonti and I had grown so close that we began to refer to each other as sisters and what soon ensued was a relationship in comparison to the one of David, King of Israel, and Jonathan, son of Saul in the Bible. We were so congruent at times that we were able to predict one another's thoughts and finish each other's sentences. Our spirits were truly kindred and no one and nothing was strong enough to break the bond we shared.

One day, I foolishly decided to test the love she had for me. I wanted to see how genuine it was and if it would stick around for real and never leave. It's not that she even had to prove her love for me, because she had not given any reason for me to question it. I was broken still and didn't want the inconvenience of feeling vulnerable, so I proceeded with my plan. It had to be something unexpected, but executed in such an intentional fashion that it would cause her to doubt our loyalty and inflict a twinge of bitter resentment. As much as I knew she anticipated our daily interactions, I chose to ignore her for a full day. When I went to work, she greeted me with the same excitement and big grin. I rejected her. I walked past her without acknowledging her kind gestures. I could see she was stunned and a worried look crossed her face.

Sometime later she gave it another shot, assuming I was having a bad day. She flung the door of the nursery open, stood and grinned, and said loudly, "Hey Miss! How are you today?" I kept entertaining the infant I had in my arms. Her spirit was becoming worn. I started feeling terrible for this cruel game I was playing but I had to know if the friendship and love we had was real, so regrettably I continued. After a few more failed attempts to get me to speak to her, let alone acknowledge her, it was soon time for her to go home. I remember so vividly that she was extremely wounded by my actions. She dragged slowly out of the facility with her head bowed. My heart dropped, but I didn't run behind her to say that I was sorry and beg her forgiveness. Instead, I allowed the game to play on through the night and into the next day. Oh, how I wish I could get that moment back, just to set her heart and mind free and explain why I felt the need to play this sick game on someone who showed nothing but authenticity and devotion!

"I'm going to have to have surgery. There's some type of growth that's causing me discomfort and I need surgery for it," she said when she started a dialogue with me.

"*Surgery*? Nothing *major*, right," I responded frantically.

"Nah. I do have to go to the hospital, but nothing major. I can get it done through outpatient," she replied reassuringly.

"Oh, OK."

Just her words alone and not sensing any fear on her part, helped me to feel at ease. She had convinced me that everything would be just fine.

Surgery had gone well and Teonti went to be under her grandmother's care until she could return to work. The entire staff made plans to visit her on the upcoming Saturday. We all decided that we would stop at a local store and pick up a few groceries for Ms. Gillette and her grandmother. While there we became frantic about the things we thought she needed. Items were continually being piled into a basket as we canvassed every aisle while giddy chatter could be heard by some saying, "Oooh, we should get this!" and "I think she may need that!" Everyone was eager to participate to make sure that Teonti was covered and would want for nothing. Suddenly, midway down the aisle the Spirit of God spoke to me and I froze in my tracks. "She's not going to need all of this," I exclaimed.

"Whaaa…what you mean?" questioned one.

"Yeah, why won't she need all of this," another staff member asked.

By this time everyone had halted the erratic grocery spree and we all stood in the middle of the aisle as if we were in a huddle.

"Yeah, she's not going to need any of this, I just know it. I feel it," I sincerely explained.

"Oh, OK," another had responded. They all had previous experiences of the Spirit speaking to me, yet some believed and others did not. The ones that believed heeded the instruction because intuitively they knew this time was no different. They didn't question it; they just moved in response and began putting some things back where they belonged.

The mood had turned somber for a few moments as we proceeded to the checkout counter. Soon we were back on the van, traveling to see our dear friend. We arrived within 10 minutes, pulled up in the yard, parked, and prayed, not only for her strength but our own and went in.

As we entered the home, we found Ms. Gillette sitting on a couch in the living room, with a towel draped over her left shoulder tinged with spots of blood. The area that had been operated on appeared to be seeping just a bit. Everyone smiled and said their hellos and extended their well wishes as we sat on the couches closest to her. She tried to crack a smile but reminded us that she was still experiencing slight discomfort and we responded accordingly.

I sat adjacent to her. The Spirit of God was not through dealing with me. As I sat quietly and listened to the different conversations that were going on around me, the Holy Spirit caused me to remain quiet. The only thing that I was allowed to do was be still and watch. As I obeyed, there it was—the cloud!

"Oh, God, no!" I attempted to reason this occurrence in my mind. Plain as day, the cloud and its transparency was there, resting over the face of my single, dearest friend. My spirit sunk in disbelief as I was reminded of the final meeting of the Bible besties, David and Jonathan. As David took flight to the fields on the outskirts of a nearby city to escape the vile plans of death that Saul had promised to fulfill because of his immense hatred and jealously of him, Jonathan, Saul's son was too fond of David to allow his father to complete his mission. Jonathan had promised to show David a sign in the field to alert him to whether it was safe to return home or flee to another city. Jonathan's love would not allow him to see the death of his dear friend, so he gave a warning to David. After the sign had been shown to David, they both met in the field and embraced one last time and made a binding covenant with one another.

Here I was right in the middle of my own David and Jonathan experience. I had my sign, but I initially rejected it because I did not want to accept the truth of it. The truth of it was that my best friend could not return to her earthly home, but rather had to leave and go far away and this would be our last time embracing and seeing one another.

Heaven only knows what she made of my silence that day, as this was not a part of any cruel joke as before. No tears were shed that day, nor was there any gloom, just silence. As I continued to look at the cloud upon her face, my heart and mind raced uncomfortably for the short time that we remained there.

The ride back home was filled with conversations about the visit and how we prayed she would return to work soon because we all missed her. Unengaged from the conversations, I followed the tracks of grass alongside the road as we traveled and I blankly stared out of the window. I was internally trying to figure out whether my mind was playing insensitive tricks on me or was God again preparing me for an impending, boding event.

It was Sunday morning and everything seemed new. The service had ended and people were going around doing their normal greeting when two staff members found and approached me.

"Did you hear what happened to Ms. Gillette?" one asked, without apparent emotion.

"No," I replied, puzzled.

By this time I began to see other staff members who were members of our church gather around. I looked into their faces for answers, but found none.

"Ms. Gillette's grandmother called and said that she died this morning, around 5 o'clock," one said.

I shook my head slowly in disbelief.

"Yeah, she said Ms. Gillette got up early to go to the bathroom and just fell dead. She thinks she must have had a heart attack." The words seemed to drift and became inaudible.

"OK…." I turned to walk away but became temporarily immobile and abruptly the news registered then hit me like a ton of bricks! I grabbed my stomach and began to wail. It felt like the wind had been knocked out of me and I was unable to maintain my composure. I could not believe this. My best friend was gone! I could not run to the phone and dial her number to ask her to console me over the news I had just received *about her*. Like David, I had run out of earthly options, became weary, and longed for a pavilion where I could hide, so I swiftly ran to the Rock that was higher than I and found immediate rest. God proved to be the only one who could give rest to this wearied soul and bequeath the kind of peace that transcended my understanding. So with the support of other friends and reliance on God, the transition wasn't as hard or painful as it could have been and would have been without them.

As I continued to grow in God and in the things of God, He readily showed me the purpose of the gifts He had placed in me. I learned to be more sensitive to the Spirit and its leading. Whenever the Spirit led me to bless others for whatever reasons, I completed the task. Whenever I was led to pray for specific people, I obeyed. Countless encounters could be recalled to verify compliance to what the Spirit moved me to say and do, but there was one, nearly tragic time that I did not and it almost cost me my life!

It was April 2004 and two months prior, I had become engaged. Plans were being made for an impending August wedding of the same year. There were just a few months left to solidify everything and to secure venues, people, and intended guests. The first order of business was to explore suitable wedding dresses with reasonable prices.

Raising two growing girls alone with occasional assistance from my parents, it was going to be impossible to financially meet the expense of a wedding that was mediocre at best. My stepmother agreed to help with the purchase of my dress, which I accepted, and my father footed the remainder of the expenses, so my wedding worries had soon dissipated.

It was Friday evening. I worked nights and was preparing to go to work later on when the Spirit nudged me. This was a recognizable, familiar nudge and I began to weep inconsolably. The Spirit warned that something dreadful and injurious would happen and He told me that it would happen the following day, which was the Saturday that I would travel to find my wedding dress.

"What's wrong? Why do you keep crying?" asked my fiancé' with concern.

"Something bad is going to happen," I sobbed.

"What? What's going to happen?" he prodded.

"I don't know exactly *what*, but I know that something *will*...and it's going to happen tomorrow," I muffled through streams of tears.

"Awww, babe. Maybe you're just nervous or something. There's no need to be scared...everything'll be fine," he reassured.

"No, no...no. I'm telling you, it's down in my spirit and I know something is going to happen...tomorrow," I cried.

As he held me in his arms, he visibly was shaken and concerned about what the Spirit had revealed to me. "You know you can postpone getting the dress until another Saturday, if you don't feel comfortable."

"I can't. If I back out now, my stepmother will feel that I don't want to get the dress because she offered to buy it. I really don't want to go but this is the only way I can get one. I don't want no problems with Daddy or nobody," I reasoned. Yet the words did not soothe my cause, they actually made matters worse because I was attempting to go against what the Spirit precisely told me.

My guts twisted on the inside of me. I knew what I had to do. I needed to call my stepmother and let her know that I did not want to go with her to shop for my wedding dress, for several reasons, but most importantly because the Spirit expressly had given warning against it. I reported to work and wrestled with my inner man all night long. Attempting to conjure up a sound excuse that wouldn't slight her or be the cause of an even bigger rift between us, I failed to come up with anything and reluctantly decided to keep our outing as planned.

On the drive to my parents' house that morning, my spirit was completely torn. I felt nauseous and frightened at the same time. Nothing about that morning was normal and when I arrived, everyone was prepared to go. Hoping someone would straggle along as usual, that would buy me time to make up an excuse not to go through with the trip. There was my stepmother, my two girls, Jasmine and Ashonilei, my niece Precious and myself. Each step I took toward the truck we would travel in I felt as if I was the star of one long, drawn-out horror flick. My legs were stiff and my feet shuffled as if I had lead in them. Finally, I had reached the passenger-side door, sat down in the seat, and buckled up. All the girls had piled in and we were set to go.

The truck was still parked in the driveway when my dad burst out of the front door of the house and ran through the grass. "I just want y'all to have a safe trip," he said with a smile. Before I responded back I searched his face for any signs of apprehension. That would be my cue to say what the Spirit urged me to reveal, but I read nothing. As he crossed back through the grass to go inside, my heart raced and stomach churned. The words were coming, I could feel them, but somehow they got stuck in the lump in my throat and I forced them back into the pit of my soul. I didn't want to be the cause of any discord, so on we rode.

Tired from working all night long and immediately preparing that morning for the events of the day, I grew tired. As sleepy as I was, I should have dozed off several times but my nervousness would not allow me to. Every rev of the engine, every sudden stop or change of lanes kept me paralyzed. I was tense from what the Spirit had revealed and remained cautious as we rode nearly three and a half hours away from home to look for a wedding dress.

As the day progressed and all seemed to go well, I slowly began to let my guard down and convinced myself that I had been hypersensitive to the gory feelings I'd experienced and that somehow I had interpreted the information wrong. I began to lighten up and participate in the frenzy of finding the most beautiful dress to wear because, after all, I was going to be someone's bride and would be married in four months!

After scaling several racks of dresses and modeling them for hours in the tall, ceiling-length mirrors, I decided on a dress. The top was sweetheart shaped and sheer with diamond and pearl embellishments cascading across the bodice of the dress. Because of my petite stature, I chose a princess cut that flared at the waist and trailed with a mid-length, embroidered train. What an exciting, yet tiring expedition to take on this dress shopping, but the mission was now complete and it was time to go.

Everyone was hungry by this time and we agreed to travel at least half way back to home before we stopped. This was done to justify having to travel only a short distance after a nice, satisfying meal. Exertion and a full stomach could spell trouble for anyone with the kind of itinerary we had.

After conversations about the day grew to an end with a cousin who lived in the city, we all hugged and said our goodbyes before piling into the truck, heading to our destination, home. Finding comfort again in the passenger's seat, music was lightly playing in background on the radio and my defenses were quickly wearing down. I turned around one last time to see that the girls were facing each other and entertaining themselves in the hand-slapping game of coordination, Miss Mary Mack. Neither of my girls had on seatbelts, but I was too tired to argue with them. About 20 minutes from the restaurant, I fell fast asleep.

"AAAAAAGGGHHHHH!!! ONICA!" Not fully cognizant of why I was being awakened by this gut-wrenching, shrilling scream, I was suddenly too distracted by the truck traveling rapidly over the marked tire girds embedded in the asphalt to indicate we were well beyond the median off side of the road. Two seconds later we made sudden impact with the highway sign on the right side of the road that indicated that a hospital was a fourth of a mile away. "WHOMP!" was the sound of the sign being uprooted by the speed of the truck and immediately striking the hood and shattering the windshield glass. Unable to open my eyes due to not being alert enough to respond, I suddenly realized what was happening! We were in the midst of a fast-approaching tragedy.

As my stepmother jerked the wheel and overturned it back to the left, this action caused the truck to whip out of control and began flipping. The presence of God stilled me and caused me to call on the name of Jesus! "Jesus! Jesus! Jesus! Jesus!" I quietly called. The crashing sound of glass breaking against the asphalt and the skidding of metal against the road let me know that this was real! I kept calling on Jesus! Who could rescue us? Jesus! Whose hands were our lives in? Jesus! With every flip, I called upon Him! Flipping at least seven times at over 70 mph and with each turn momentum was steadily building, as we sped to the opposite side of the road! I let my body go limp with every flip. If I attempted to go against it, I could die. "WOP!" My head crashed against the dashboard and the impact scalped me from the upper bridge of my nose near my frontal lobe back to the middle of my head. My skull was exposed and blood poured from my open wounds. The impact immediately had swollen my eyes completely shut and caused me to suffer a C3 fracture or Hangman's fracture that is identified by the type of broken necks that people who had been hanged endured.

The truck came to a halt and rested on the newly-installed cables in the middle of the road, turned on its left side. I didn't realize it then but my right arm was broken and I sat still, amazingly in NO pain, thanking God for the miracle He'd just performed. Suddenly I felt my breathing become shallow and slightly pressured, but I did not speak. I listened intently with my ears to see if I could pick up signs and sounds of life around me. Half dazed, I just started praying that my girls were OK. The extended silence began to play with my mind and I began to sense the worst. Were my babies gone? I began to panic!

Anyone who walked up on the scene could readily see that it was grim and survival from such a horrific accident appeared bleak. The first responder that contacted my dad warned that before he came to convey the mangled scenery he should expect a few fatalities, if not all that were involved. How was he able to endure the thought of all his family members suddenly being assumed dead?

Ambulances began blaring in the distance toward us. Still I sat, draining life and becoming noticeably faint as the moments slowly passed. Suddenly, a fireman called out to me to see if I was alive. My voice wasn't strong and registered barely above a strong whisper. He reached through the broken window on my side of the truck, took my pulse, called for back-up, and attempted to open the door. It was jammed shut! A call was made for the Jaws of Life to come and cut the door off and rush me to get immediate medical attention. While on the ambulance ride over to the hospital I mustered enough strength to ask where my girls were. "They're fine," someone replied. I wasn't sure if this was protocol to respond to a victim in this way, but I wasn't reassured by the tone and the delivery of the answer to the question.

We arrived to the emergency department in no time. Not able to open my eyes and observe my surroundings, I simply had to trust God that He had everything under control, aside from the fact that He had just delivered us all out of a horrible pit and performed quite a splendid miracle. Recalling the recent event, I began to thank God for hearing my cry as I called upon Him! Little 'ol, insignificant me! My spirit experienced peace and I began to relax. Soon I was reassured by a familiar voice. God was still at work! It was Joanna, a charge nurse I had worked closely with on the Behavioral Health Unit of the hospital.

"Onica? This is Joanna"! she called out in an angelic tone. "Hi, Joanna!" I responded with relief, as they proceeded to work on me. "Where are my girls?" I asked with more calm. "They're doing OK! We're taking care of them," Joanna responded soothingly. "Lord, I thank you!" I thought with extreme gratitude. "Jesus!" It mattered not what state I found myself in, it was the Lord's power and grace that caused me to rest in contentment.

As days passed and turned into weeks, I learned that my oldest girl had been ejected out of the vehicle 100 or more feet away from where the truck rested during the series of overturns then slammed onto the road in the midst of traffic, which resulted in both her legs being broken. My baby girl was ejected from the truck as well and when it finally ceased from flipping, she was found pinned underneath. As a result of the impact in which she was thrown, she suffered moderate memory loss and remembers nothing about the accident to this day.

After being placed in a medically-induced coma for facial reconstruction surgery, I remained in that state for over a week. Due to the excessive swelling and fluid on my brain, my eyes were still swollen shut and I attempted daily to pry them open. Family and friends would stop by to visit and talk, but I could only hear their voice and it bothered me that I could not lay eyes on them. Becoming more agitated by the day, I began to be uncooperative toward doctors and staff. As a result, since I had suffered a TBI (traumatic brain injury) doctors started to believe that the damage may have affected my ability to behave and follow simple instructions. I wasn't mentally impaired, I was frustrated! Nevertheless, I was transferred to the TBI unit for closer supervision. Here is where I reached my breaking point.

I had become mobile and could get up and down out of the bed with little assistance. One day in particular, I had the urge to get up and go to the bathroom. Slowly, I shuffled out of bed and onto the walker for support. With the neck brace still about my neck and my right arm in a cast, I managed to turn my head slightly to look at my likeness in the nearby mirror. I was not prepared for what I saw! I froze in my tracks and gasped for air that was getting thinner by the second. What in the world was going on? Immediately, I began to bawl. Nobody mentioned to me that my face was disfigured and destroyed! I quickly lowered my head in disbelief hoping that the image I saw was a figment of my imagination and that my eyes were still weak from the entire trauma. I gently raised my head to stare at the ugly truth that faced me. My face was deformed and resembled a grotesque, misshaped puzzle whose pieces were forced to fit. My appearance would never be the same, no matter what! Barely standing now, taking inventory of the staples, stitches, gauze, and dried blood, I observed an unrecognizable, battered person. I stood at the sink and cried! I cried for the little girl who had already struggled most of her life to be accepted, the one who had to search for an inkling of self-esteem. I wept for the young teenaged mother who felt she had to use her body to show her love to others because these were the lessons inflicted on her. I balled for the young, misguided woman who stood at the crossroads of life-altering decision making. Furthermore, I profusely wailed for her who seemingly had no resemblance to the person she was before. Even though she had some hang ups, she knew there were pleasant qualities about her that made her desirable. But who was this? I didn't know! This person was the twin of Frankenstein, one who would scare others with just one glance and one who could possibly be pre-judged as a hardened criminal due to the long gashes and scars across her face. How could I face my children? Would they still love me the same as they had before this tragedy? Frightened to entertain the possibilities, I just scooted back to bed and sobbed uncontrollably.

Depression and frustration were becoming my two traveling companions through this hospital stint. Having to endure battery of tests, both cognitive and physical, was wearing me thin. What made matters worse was the fact that I hadn't laid eyes on my children for three weeks. This was the longest span of time that I had spent away from them and it was making me sick. After tolerating all the empty promises of visiting my children from the medical staff and sustaining worrisome procedures and extensive levels of functioning tests, the day finally came when they allowed me to walk down two halls to visit my children. Seeing them would be the only thing to lift my spirits because I knew God had been a faithful Keeper. Directed by staff to a door located on the left side of the second hall, happily I found my immediate family gathered around my oldest daughter. Shockingly, she was positioned in a wheelchair close to her bed. She had been in surgery to place rods and pins in her legs to aid in her ability to eventually become mobile again. Unprepared for the prognosis of her condition, I tried to be strong for her and put on a façade, but inwardly I was conflicted and sad.

Thankfully, my baby girl had been discharged three days after the accident. She suffered a small gash on her forehead and some second-degree burns to the skin on her feet. My father had taken on the role of Mom in my stead while I recuperated. Everyone chatted and asked about our progress, which in considering the alternative was phenomenal, we weren't dead! At that very moment, God reminded me that although the situation looked hopeless and dismal at the beginning, the joy was found in knowing that we were all sustained for His mighty purpose. We made it! We were alive!

During this time of recovery I had to learn to become totally dependent on God simply because I had no one else. Here I was helpless, weak, and handicapped, not even able to bathe properly or look after my children due to the severity of the injuries I had sustained. At times the small successes of opening my eyes or walking around my room caused me to think that I was overcoming mightily in my own strength, but somehow just as quickly as I had thought it, suddenly I was reminded of the Word of God that declares His strength is made perfect in my weakness. I was really being tested from the beginning of this trial to the bitter end. God trusted me with that test of infirmity just as He had done Job and I completely let God be God. I appreciated the fact that He entrusted me with the gift to go through and recognize His sustaining power.

It was *me*, the words I spoke to my God that fateful day that saved us all, even my stepmother. The miracle of calling on the name of Jesus *in the midst* of calamity during a mighty, raging storm and He quickly answer, caused my faith to expand by leaps and bounds! The reassurance in knowing that Jesus is ever-present with us and has not forsaken us is amazing. When the storm presented itself in the form of an unbridled truck flipping carelessly through the air, Jesus stood firm and commanded the storm to cease! "Peace, be still," and immediately the truck rested.

To the enemy's detriment I survived to not only tell the story of amazing, undeserved grace but I serve as a testament and representative of God's glory and the power erected when you call on the name of Jesus. The adversary couldn't take my treasure away even in my most vulnerable moments. God protected it just as He was protecting me because He's loving, kind and good. Devil, you didn't win!

Chapter 8

This Thorn 12:7

"There was given to me a thorn in the flesh, the messenger of Satan to buffet me, lest I should be exalted above measure."

The entire relationship started out wrong. I had heard enough sermons and knew enough Word (the Bible) to know that what was birthed out of sin would eventually come to naught. The fact that he was separated and not yet divorced from his second wife should have been enough evidence to confirm that this relationship was on the fast track to pain and despair. But when you decide to waltz through portions of your life wearing rose-colored lenses, your true intuitions, reasoning and vision becomes extremely and dangerously clouded.

It's amazing how we know at times the ending of a story before we've actually *read* the entire thing. Oftentimes, we also take for granted that which is clearly stated in God's Word as consequences to deliberate sin or misbehavior and go to the extent of co-signing onto and keeping the parts of His Word that we agree with while tossing out what is intolerable to our rebellious natures. Moreover, we would rather subscribe to falsehoods of thinking that what is concretely defined as marked boundaries against God's Word and contrary to His way allows for alterations, substitutions and exceptions.

Because God is sovereign and has no respect of persons, what He says of one He applies to all for His Word is literally all-inclusive, meaning that no matter how saved you are or how far you think you've come, none of us are exempt from every consequence of poor choice. Be not deceived, God is not mocked; that which you have sown, you shall also reap.

I was 26 years old, a single mother with two young daughters who were 10 and 7. Unfortunately, neither of their fathers were actively participating or parenting in their lives. My back was against a wall and all the odds appeared to be stacked against me concerning the fear of finding a suitable mate who would consider me becoming a wife, as if that were some grand accomplishment. Nobody seemed to want or desire a single woman that came with a complete, ready-made family. I remember being told often that I should just settle for whatever I could get and that my expectations should not appear to be so high. As long as the suitor could maintain a job and not have violent tendencies, everything else seemed negotiable. My self-esteem had plummeted over the years so by this time despite being a newly-converted Christian, present circumstances did not hold any foreshadowing evidence of brighter days.

I was in and out of dead-end relationships that literally had no promise of success from the start. Either the guy had a rather colorful personality or possessed the ability to simply keep me entertained or they were not much farther along than I was in life, but had a job and with a lot of grooming, slight potential to be something greater in the future. My standards were mediocre and I did not require much more than for the individual to make me feel wanted or desired. I really just wanted someone to love me and call me their own, nothing more, nothing less. Here I was, broken and seeking.

Everything seen seemed to be the right remedy or cure for someone like me with a deadly diagnosis of shattered vision and a fragmented heart. How would I know what was really good for me when I was looking through eyes that were guided by an inoperative spirit and soul void of discernment? For sure I needed God's help, all the signs were there, but I mistakenly assumed that I could handle this one by myself. After all, it was *my* heart and I knew *what* I needed and *who* I needed to help fix it. A word of caution here: Anytime you feel the urge to help God out, don't! You will only prolong the lessons that extend your route toward your destiny. Whatever you placed in your own hands and have done in your own strength will ultimately fail; undoubtedly, undeniably, every single time.

There wasn't a whole lot that I knew prior to this encounter about this man other than the fact that we attended the same church, he was an ordained Deacon and a man of God appearing as an angel of light. Before now, nothing but short-spanned occurrences of sporadically passing each other on Sundays is all we shared. Initially there existed a mutual attraction and the romance began much like any other, except I was aware of the fact that he wasn't fully a "free" man.

Our first real chance meeting was quite an interesting one. A puzzling, yet intriguing conversation struck up after Bible Study one evening between the two of us. I was headed toward my car when I heard my name being called by a voice that I did not recognize, so I quickly turned in response. What happened next caught me completely by surprise. "So how'd you like Bible study tonight," he asked.

"Oh, I enjoyed it," I responded enthusiastically.

"Can I ask you a question?"

At this point I assumed we would expound on what we had just been taught in the Word. To my surprise, it wasn't that at all. He proceeded, "If I were to become single, do you think I would have a chance?"

Instantly taken aback, I thought, *Wait, what?*" The smile I had was quickly being turned into a grimace of embarrassment. This question had me stunned, until finally I could mumble a few audible words. "Uhhhmmm, I believe so...yeah, I guess...why?"

Now I was completely disconcerted. As hypothetical as I wanted to believe this leading question was, the meaning of it could go well beyond the boundaries for what is normally acceptable for first encounters between two individuals. Nonetheless, suddenly a seed of anticipation and destruction had simultaneously been planted in both of our minds and eventually with time and opportunity, the fruition of sin began its steady, dishonest weaving of a treacherous, tangled web.

All of the players were equally vested in this game of love and loss; each one was seeking something different from the other. What I desired most was to *be* loved and *feel* loved and he constantly battled infinite thoughts of insecurity and hardly ever sensed that he measured up or was enough like he had something to prove. Hopeless from the start, these issues presented additional unique challenges for us because it is always difficult to create something meaningful and long-lasting when these self-defeating obstacles are constantly creating barriers, aside from the rebellious sinful nature of this bond. The two of us felt invincible, as if we had this entire journey all planned out. It seemed to be us against the world at the onset, but just as people had readily believed that the Earth was flat until explorers refuted the myth and proved them wrong, we had major misconceptions about our own connection with each other.

There was a time in my life where I had created quite a list of things that I would never do or be accused of doing and being entangled with a married man was one of the top three. I knew that morally it was wrong and was cognizant of the possible consequences behind this choice. Although people choose to involve themselves in these types of situations willingly, there ultimately are no winners, but rather causalities of war. I call it war because someone is fighting another individual for what they claim or consider being theirs. The enemy knows just how to tempt us and understands that the stakes are so high that he's allowed only a fragment of time to present illusions of concealed truth to ultimately carry us blindly away. He's been an expert of his craft since the beginning of time as evidenced in the Garden of Eden.

There's no gain for him to waste time on things and people that you don't desire or are not tempted by, whether secretly or through open confession. Even in our thoughts, he works overtime to convince us that certain beliefs we hold whether morally or spiritually are either completely wrong or misguided. His ultimate goal is to have us question the validity of what we believe and know to be true then he proceeds to usher us into a place of compromise. This is why it remains vitally important to guard our minds as well as our hearts at all cost and be vigilant about obtaining and keeping the mind of Christ without fail.

Four months after the accident, our wedding proceeded as scheduled. During the months prior, I spent a lot of time struggling to recuperate, not only my physical body but mentally as well. Questions of self-worth constantly plagued me due to the fact that my world had literally been altered in many ways and appearances were amplified and meant everything. I wanted to present myself as beautifully as I had always dreamed I would as a bride, but something was intensely wrong! I wasn't the type of bride that I had envisioned being. There was nothing pure, lovely, or chaste about me. Although I wasn't the cause of breaking up a marriage, I played a significant background role that led to thoughts of anticipating a promising new life. Now left with feelings of regret of the pain and turmoil I caused not only to myself but to others as well, I began to slowly fall apart.

It was 1 o'clock and the wedding day was here. I would be married in one hour. The conviction of the Holy Spirit was heavy that day and was beginning to deal with me mightily. I became very nervous and nearly nauseous thinking about the series of events due to happen in the next several hours. As the makeup was being applied to my face, I scanned my mind to think of ways to escape and retreat to an undisclosed place far away. Away from having to stand in my truth and make serious decisions that would alter life as I had become accustomed to with this man I did not completely love. Knowing this was impossible to do, I looked for signs to lead me into what to say and do at this point. This was the first time I had to face something so life-changing that I had spent so much time preparing for. What was going on and why did I sense such unrest? I was supposed to be happy and excited about this day and the ordeal that was quickly approaching. I began to show signs of anxiety and wanted to run and cry. Suddenly, I needed Daddy! Where was Daddy? He could bring calm to this storm I was experiencing! His comforting words of wisdom would soothe me and cause me to ponder on what was impending with a clearer heart and conscious, but he couldn't be reached because he was already positioned at the Church making sure everything there was in order. I was quickly malfunctioning emotionally, growing increasingly out of whack by the second, and needed him now.

The limo pulled up to Daddy's house and my stomach dropped. This was really happening. As I climbed into the high, cushioned seat and attempted to make myself as comfortable as possible, I caught news on the radio that a hurricane was ensuing and would be approaching the area soon. It was sunny on the outside with just a hint of cloud here and there, but I knew what was brewing. Intuitively, I felt just like this broadcast of breaking news. It was foreboding the forecast of my soul; a beautiful bride on the outside but inwardly, deeply conflicted.

The ride to the church seemed extremely long as I gazed out of the window thinking about how much my life was getting ready to change, not for the better but for the worse. All I needed at this point was for someone to stop me and tell me that the unction I was feeling was not wrong and that maybe this was not the right thing to have happen at this time. I became scared all over again. Slowly pulling into the church and seeing the parking lot full of cars driven by the well-wishers, I began apologizing in my mind to them all. I didn't want to be here and I wasn't allowing the Spirit to take complete control. Lots of time and money had been spent to make this day possible. There was no chance of any refunds being given back, it was too late, or so I thought. Boy was the enemy working my mind overtime in finding reason to proceed and finally compromise with this fiasco.

Everyone was in place and anxiously anticipating the start of the festivities. I totally ignored the bridesmaids' expressions of awe when I entered the room where they were waiting. Some cried in amazement while others approvingly smiled. I, on the other hand, just wanted counsel from my dad. So my responses were given with a stoned effect.

The ceremony began and everything was performed like rehearsed. Finally, my dad came to the room to escort me to the entrance of the sanctuary's doors. "You ready," he asked with a huge smile. "It's time!"

I studied his eyes, long and hard to see if I could read the slightest bit of hesitation. Disappointed, I found none and reluctantly answered, "Yes," with a plastered smile. I waited for him to give that last piece of advice of, "If you're having second thoughts about this, you don't have to go through with it" or his famous, "What did *God* say," but neither were heard, at least not audibly. I believe this was loudly being played in my mind and his proud stance and smile began to cause that voice to fade. Just then the doors opened and as a last resort, I jerked onto Daddy's arm so that he could feel my hesitation. The closer our steps came to approaching the altar, the tighter my grip became. I wanted to turn around, now! The pride Daddy displayed of a King walking his Princess down the corridor to be met with her Prince did not allow for him to recognize or feel the desperate tug on his arm or silent cry for help and as a result, I felt doomed. I had arrived at the point of no return!

The ceremony progressed onward and Daddy stood to give his agreement for us to become one. Here was the serious part, the segment where we would say our vows, before God and man. Just seven days earlier after a serious falling out between us, I suggested that we rethink this entire situation and not get married, but here we stood, face to face in the presence of all of our eager guests. With confidence he recited his vows to me, as I looked on with amazement. Then it was my turn to echo what was being asked of me to recite, and unexpectedly I lost it! Right in the middle of pronouncing my vows, I realized the weight of the words that I was speaking and began to cry. How could I stand before God and lie? My mouth formed the words, but my heart and soul discerned the truth.

Onlookers assumed that I was crying because this was known to be the most sacred part of the ceremony; however this was far from accurate for me! If they had an inkling of what I desired to do at this moment they would be greatly angered and let down. Soon embarrassment settled in and jolted me into a place of numbness. Now, I just wanted to get this sideshow of a wedding over with!

The weather outside had drastically changed from when I first arrived and it seemed that just as we had finished saying our vows to one another, the storm came. There suddenly was a downpour of rain and dark clouds filled the sky. By the time the wedding party was due to file out of the church, we were cautioned to remain inside due to the surrounding streets becoming flooded. There was no clear way to safely travel to the next venue for the reception, so we waited until conditions became clearer. Sadly in retrospect, this entire scenario was indeed foreboding to what the marriage itself would unfold in due time. Astonishingly, there would be numerous, tumultuous storms to weather and just as many dark clouds to attempt to dissipate.

Resentment of being married had already crept inside me before night came. Trying to mask the reality of what I felt inwardly, outwardly I started to show signs of impatience and blatant agitation. Feelings of regret had overtaken me, even feelings of being lost and having nowhere to turn. As a result, I rehearsed having a serious conversation about annulment of the marriage with my newly-wed husband. After mulling it over a few times in my mind, the time came for me to verbalize all that my soul was concealing and it was easier than I had thought it would be.

As soon as I stood in my confidence the words just poured out, "I think I made a big mistake." A paralyzing silence filled the room and apparent sadness swept over his face. Questions of how I could feel this way and who or what was influencing me to express these things came flooding in.

"My spirit has been in turmoil all day and it was too late to change my mind because everything was paid for!"

I was crying now because I felt like an innocent incarcerated person that was declared guilty but had one last shot to plead his case. "I just don't want to be married no more. I made a big mistake! All we have to do is get it annulled. I just can't...."

Keeping back the nauseous sensations that were rapidly bubbling up, I curled up in a ball on one side of the bed we were sharing and made sure there was no closeness between us that would encourage intimacy. Sex was the furthest thought from my mind. There was no way I could bring myself to officially consummate this marriage, so I didn't. It would be well over a month before that happened and truly then it was somewhat out of obligation.

Infidelity entered into the marriage before the initial six months of this new life had expired. Between the two of us there was a good mix of unmet needs, neglect, lack of quality time and attention and no shortage of others from the outside that willingly rendered themselves, as well as purposely desired to satisfy each of us at any cost. The tables had really turned. At the onset, we vowed to make it work even through the threats of getting an annulment or divorcing. Emotionally dead and beginning to seek outside attention, some days were harder in trying to keep that promise than others. For the most part, all of my indiscretions were secretly done to an extent, whereas his were poorly planned or performed and was readily discovered. There were accounts where numbers were found in the pockets of pants in the laundry with names written on them. Then there were guys listed in my phone under female names that went unnoticed. Soon the weight of all the dishonesty began to bother me and ate away at my conscience when I thought about all that I was doing not only to him, but to God. Even if I wasn't in love with this man I still wanted to be in right standing with God.

I figured that disclosing all that I did outside the marriage would appease him and coerce him to appreciate the fact that I had the courage to tell him then I expected him to find it in his heart to forgive me. I had crossed the line and got involved in an emotional affair that was at the brink of escalating into something bigger and potentially more deadly. I thought he would be remorseful for every single time that I begged for his time and attention and he chose to divide them deeper into his work and different hobbies. I'd hope that he recognized that I had grown tired of the same boring routines and lack of luster in our married life and just needed to be refreshed or restored.

Maybe he'd understand that a marriage couldn't be built off of sporadic conversations and random acts of sex. *If I told him, maybe he would see my heart and know that I really wanted to work things out and move forward,* I thought. But I was dead wrong! I decided to tell him everything and as soon as I did, he became irate. I explained that nothing was done to hurt him intentionally but rather for him to see that I was really suffering from the ways things were between us. *I could have just kept on going...he wouldn't have known,* I reasoned in my mind. But *I* would have known and so would God. Now that my soul was released from bondage, I found myself trying to pick up the pieces of my now fragmented marriage. He moved out the next week and we were officially separated.

We had talked about having children together, and since he had none, we tried for three years and still produced no child. We visited my gynecologist whose diagnosis was that I wouldn't bear any more children. Furthermore, the fertility specialist declared that his count was so low that it would be impossible to impregnate me. Truth is, I never believed either report, and had firmly believed the promise that God had distinctly given to me, but the fact that we were separated without intentions of reconciling made chances of us having any children together impossible.

The next year without financial stability, emotional stability, and having only a shimmer of spiritual stability made the highs and lows of life seem so much more magnified. To add to this unbearable stress, my estranged husband called one day out of the blue four months post-separation to inform me that his new girlfriend was pregnant and they were expecting a boy. My heart sank and I thought, *God, you really know how to place vengeance on somebody.* Hearing the news made me depressed and angry and I could not stop crying. *How is it that You blessed them to have a child, a boy at that? That was my heart's desire, that's what I wanted with my husband.* The devil taunted me to no end! He had me questioning my womanhood and why I couldn't produce any more children, he brought into question how my husband was able to make babies now without me, he even played with my mind to have me compare myself to the other woman and seemingly on all fronts, I didn't measure up.

For a few weeks the enemy had me in his grip. I continued to cry out to God to take my heart and mend all the fragmented pieces and make me whole again. Soon when the Spirit could get my undivided attention, He led me back to one of the Scriptures that has effectively led me through turbulent times found in Psalms 34:18 NLT where it reads, "The Lord is close to the brokenhearted; He rescues those whose spirits are crushed." My spirit was crushed and indeed, He proved to be closer to me than I was able to physically sense. Not only that, but he *came* for me! When I was lost and ashamed, subjectively bound in a horrible pit, He came for me and He *rescued* me. This demonstrates a loving attribute of His as Savior. He saves, rescues and delivers those in danger and difficulty.

Months went by and my resilience was returning stronger than ever. Increasing time spent in my prayer life helped me to foster some peace about this life-altering event. I found myself asking incisive questions about the impending pregnancy, how things were coming along, and what future plans my estranged husband had for his newly-formed family. He always responded indecisively and never wanted to entertain the notion of ending our marriage. He seemed somewhat excited over his girlfriend's pregnancy and looked forward to having a son to the extent of buying all the necessary equipment for its arrival. This was extremely hard to witness, but what could I do? Confused, I began to search for information to find out more about the girlfriend and the validity of this pregnancy. As the saying goes seek and ye shall find. I found a lot more than I had bargained for and the results were not comely.

I dug deep and recalled a very significant chance conversation with the girlfriend where I was expressing to her how this whole situation had been affecting me. She explained how they met and when the relationship had begun. To my surprise it had started before I confessed my sins to my husband about the indiscretions that I committed and discovered they were just the catalyst he needed to validate his leaving. She continued to come clean about everything. The similarities of her and my meeting and connecting with my husband were mind boggling! She too was hit with the "If I weren't married, would I have a chance" line! And like me, she fell for it.

She expressed how she had never been married but desperately desired to be one day. The closest she had come to anything that resembled marriage was a long-standing live-in relationship with the father of her children that ended after several years. She spoke of her daughters and how she later in life decided that she wanted more children but divulged to me that she couldn't because she'd gotten her tubes tied. At the time I revealed that my husband and I were trying to have children but could not and that although I was angry about the entire situation of wanting to be the one to give my husband something he never had by bearing his children and how I considered the opportunity to now be stolen from me, I still wished them well.

Men can be so gung-ho sometimes that they often don't pay attention to detail or ask the poignant questions needed to gather insight, rather they go along with whatever is initially presented to them. This was the case for my estranged husband. I'd remembered the conversation that the girlfriend and I had about her inability to produce any more children, so as the "pregnancy" progressed, I asked probing questions to him. Had he been to any doctor's visits or been given any proof that the pregnancy existed? No. Did he recognize any signs of pregnancy such as morning sickness, fatigue or weight gain? No. I asked more and more questions to persuade him to get the answers he needed for himself and his family that knew about the situation. I already knew and discerned that there was no pregnancy, but I didn't force my hand, I just sat back and watched the tale unfold. On the contrary, there was a positive pregnancy test that soon surfaced. Shocked and disenchanted, I remained vigilant on the strength of the information that was divulged to me.

The time came about that the nine month tenure of pregnancy should end and everyone's nerves were on edge. My estranged husband's anxiety shot through the roof as he was preparing to become a father. It had been a long span of time seemingly, and his wait was about to be over. There was a call made to him that his girlfriend had been in the hospital but was now at home resting. He asked why he wasn't called when she was in active labor pending delivery while at the hospital. She informed him that because everything happened so quickly unfortunately she lost the baby and that it was delivered stillborn. Distraught and in disbelief, he began a downward spiral emotionally and reached out to the only constant in his life, me. As I attentively listened to his regrets, woes, and apologies I convinced him to find out details about the hospital visit to see if protocol was followed in failing to notify him as the untimely events were unfolding.

When he called the hospital it was found that there had been a recent visit from his girlfriend, only the visit was related to an elevated, unmaintained blood pressure issue. There had been no delivery, no baby and no pregnancy! Infuriated, he demanded answer that would explain why he had been strung along for so long without a clue as to what was really going on. She then revealed that the roundness of her belly these past months had been created by a pillow and girdle. As for the positive pregnancy test that was produced, she brought to light that she had gone through the elaborate process of getting one of her close friends, who was expecting, to urinate in a container so that she could later use it to seal the deal on this deception. All of this was done in efforts to keep him, create a family with him and to eventually get married to him. Although everything was done in vain and ultimately to cause emotional harm to me and my family, ironically this would not be the end of their connection to one another, despite the fact that he was wounded deeply by the elaborate games.

A short time expired and my estranged husband and I decided to forgive all transgressions committed against one another and move forward in rekindling and repairing our marriage. The timing couldn't have been any better for God knew what was in the workings and the manifestations of His promises were on the brink of being fulfilled. Three weeks into our reunion, my husband received the abrupt, unfortunate news that his father had unexpectedly died of a massive heart attack while sitting in his truck prepared to begin his workday. A sheriff had been attempting to get in contact with my husband all day at his job while he ran his route with his company truck. His boss tried to convince him to stop his workday early because they needed to share some news with him.

Surprised by the wording of his boss' statement and without knowing details he began calling me to make sure that I was OK. I reassured him that I was fine and inquired about his sudden anxiety. He explained that his boss said that a sheriff needed to speak with him concerning one of his family members. Soon after, he called his mom and siblings. They all reported doing well. Then he arrived back at work to see the sheriff waiting to tell him the news. Confused, he approached the inside of the building where his boss and the sheriff cautiously stood and released the news. Broken and scared, I was the first person he called. He slowly revealed why his boss was so adamant about him returning to work early and what details the sheriff had disclosed. Immediately we traveled to the hospital where his father's remains were and began making arrangements.

The Bible speaks in John 12:24 MSG of a grain of wheat that is buried in the ground and that if it does not die, it alone is never but a grain of wheat. This Scripture goes on to explain that if this seed is released in love and buried it will sprout and reproduce itself many times over. As a matter of fact, the results of it will be with you forever and it will be real and eternal. Not to insinuate that all deaths are joyous events but all do have purpose. Truthfully, as we were burying my husband's father and releasing one life in love, another life was being formed in love the very same day! Our promise and miracle of a baby boy was now being placed in motion to come to fruition. Two weeks later, my pregnancy was confirmed and I was elated. On the other hand, this news took my husband by surprise and doubt settled in.

Doubt has a way of being counterproductive in the presence of miracles. Because of my husband's unforeseen, negative reaction to the pregnancy, I started to feel down and initially questioned why this was happening. So overjoyed over the wonder that had taken place, I forgot about the not-so-recent past of the illegitimate, fake pregnancy of the girlfriend and how emotionally drained he had been over it. I didn't think that one had anything to do with the other, but where he was concerned, it did. In the beginning of my pregnancy I had to go above and beyond to prove that I was indeed pregnant to the extent of taking multiple tests in front of him. Soon the constant reassuring became taxing and overbearing. Not understanding how this miracle could invoke so many different emotions on the intended parties, I reached out to God for the answers. What would be revealed through the Spirit would be astonishing.

He was the only child of his father, which made him sole beneficiary of his late father's estate. Initially he was excited over the possibilities of things he could buy with the money he had received. One of his desires was to purchase a brand-new motorcycle equipped with all the latest features of comfort and style, but his recent mismanagement of his inheritance shortened the finances needed to make this possible. Furthermore, the thought of having to use a portion of his money to now prepare for a child caused him to act unseemly. Newly pregnant and realizing the need for preparation of a baby, he made rash decisions that placed us in formidable circumstances. His desire for materialistic things was so strong that he quickly sought a way to finance a brand- new bike. After it was revealed that we could not afford this venture, he became ill and disturbingly emotionally abusive.

Consequently, I sunk deeper into an emotional, downward spiral. Inwardly, I was ecstatic about the promise growing inside me, but I dared not express it outwardly around him. With every harsh word thrust against me, I clung even tighter to My Help because I needed solace and rest from these senseless acts. Sometimes the undue stress and pressure was so intense that I resolved in my mind that he was intentionally setting up circumstances to make me lose our baby. To further confirm this, he'd planned a nice getaway to celebrate our wedding anniversary, only to unexpectedly a week later abandon both me and his unborn child. We hadn't fussed or disagreed about anything prior to this selfish act, nevertheless I was left alone and confused to bear the weight of this trauma all by myself. Later, the truth began to unfold once again because he had reconnected once more with the girlfriend he'd just dismissed a few short months prior and now resided with her.

Emotionally, here I was, gasping for air that seemed a bit insufficient in an environment that was rapidly smothering me. How could he leave me at a time like this? Moreover, in spite of any difficulty we may have been facing, how could he abandon a promise from Almighty God, a promise that was manifested amidst fiery trials and unpredictable tribulations? I was angry because the answers weren't coming as fast as I would have liked them to nor were they making any sense and with each passing day it appeared that he was happy being with the female who had just stolen from him this opportunity of producing a new life through the faked-out pregnancy. My back was pressed against a wall again and only the blessing of becoming chosen to carry this promise of God to term made me strongly persevere. There was no way that I would be counted incapable of completing this divine assignment!

And it came to pass that I bore my first son, a symbol of promise, whose name was derived from Abraham and Sarah's son named Isaac, which means "laughter." Twenty months later, I bore my second son of promise whose name means "strength" that is derived from Caleb who was the confident companion of Joshua sent by Moses to survey the new land that would become the promised property of God's chosen remnant, the Israelites. In honoring God, I earnestly prayed to carefully choose names for both of my sons that would bring His name glory. As Hannah, Samuel the prophet's mother in the Old Testament had prayed for a son and vowed to give him back to God for His service, I too took the same oath. I realized that for all the Hell I had endured in the waiting phase of receiving these vessels of assurance through separation, abandonment, ridicule, abuse and exploitation, every ounce of it was necessary and worthy for its production.

Although the marriage dissolved and there remains reoccurring themes of abandonment where my sons are concerned, the two most important things that I was literally left with by my former husband were Laughter and Strength. He may have taken several tangible things and even invoked some great emotional cavities, what remains is far greater than what was! I can celebrate the fact that the JOY of the Lord has been my STRENGTH. This thorn never could have killed me because it wasn't designed to do so, but it only came to humble me and for His glory to be ensued in the Earth as testament to His unmerited favor upon my life.

Celebrate your thorns! Every rose is surrounded by them, but its beauty outshines them all, causing the thorns to fade and become unrecognizable, giving glory to its Maker.

Chapter 9

Causing Us to Triumph 2:14

"Now thanks be unto God, which always causeth us to triumph in Christ, and maketh manifest the savior of his knowledge by us in every place."

    When we look at a tree, we only see the portion of it that is above ground. Most of us at first glance would have no idea about the condition of its roots, what circumstances it required to get underway and what it suffered to become stable and grow. To study the genesis of the tree means to go back to its origin and study all components involved for its development to foster a vast understanding of the stories of glory and grace a tree personifies.

    Way before trees are erected, each had their beginning inside a seed. Seeds vary in sizes and shapes and are cased in an outer covering of protection. Most interestingly, what is known is that everything the tree would become was already contained within its seed. Although the initial phases of growth can't be detected or seen, something is happening underneath the ground. There is a process that the seed must submit to in order to achieve its destiny to full capacity.

    Like the seed, we too must submit to our personal processes to invoke advancement. Germination takes place during the darkest of moments, but the seed pulls heavily on what lies inside of itself to accelerate progression. Indeed, dark moments are what define and test the tenacity of our strength. Without them, fear would continue to grapple us and cause us to remain in comfortable and ungodly places, situations and circumstances. Being in the dark a second longer than purposed drives us to search for the light. When light comes and all goes well the aftermath of the seed following its stages of growth or maturity is the production of a tree. Depending upon how the tree had the ability to flourish and surpass its predicted course of progression or become measurably useful relies mostly on the seed. What condition was the seed in before it was planted? Was the soil suitable and viable enough to foster its intended development? Without knowing the answers to these questions based solely on observation, one must dig a little deeper to find what is sometimes hidden in plain view.

Seeds are very powerful things. Although most start out small, insignificant and unassuming, the potential each has is enormous! They have the ability to expand and yield something more massive than its initial seedling. Jesus confirmed this principle through the teaching of a mustard seed in Matthew 17:20 and correlated the size of it to the faith needed to make miracles happen. He taught that if any would have the faith the size of a mustard seed that we could accomplish great things through possessing something so minute and small. Amazingly, seeds that are planted today have in them the promise to become a forest tomorrow, but only after taking care and planting them in grounds that are productive.

Before I became a seed in my mother's womb, God foreknew me. In eternity's past I began as a thought of God, preset with purpose and intention. Everything that I was envisioned to become and had ever hoped of being was already inside of me. As a tender seed it was apparent that some handicaps and utter misfortunes were thrust upon me causing the potential of my soil to become contaminated, tainted, and useless. Nevertheless, through it all, God caused me to triumph! That means He pushed me into victory!

Seeds in their infancy must have the necessary environment and nutrients to flourish properly. By nature, seeds have affinities for water that are embedded into soil. Once the water is found, the seed finds its stability inside the soil and become roots. Secondly, the seed will open up and seek after the sunlight. It extends itself by reaching for the sun's rays to eventually become branches and leaves. Meanwhile, the seed doesn't even recognize that the very thing it was set to thrive in had just as much opposition surrounding it too. Other seeds compete for food, water and their spot in the sunlight. This is why many seeds are planted but very few grow to maturity. Many are called, but only few are chosen!

Depending upon the kind of seed, each are planted in different seasons. The reason is because the season in which they are planted holds the right balance of conditions needed to see growth take place. The sunlight is just right, as well as the temperature surrounding the seed and accessibility of the water that the seed craves; all of these are brought in and by its season. The various seasons I've been exposed to have evoked growth in me that I never thought possible!

Though I've had to endure several harsh Winter seasons where long-running relationships suddenly turned bitterly brisk and cold, to the extent of my well-intending, ever-nourishing leaves becoming extensively brittle, dry and dead, I had to shed these people, circumstances and things to replace the hurtful barrenness I bore in order for spring to be welcomed to usher in a newness that could not be explained. As the seasons changed, God never did. Even as I continued to evolve, God remained consistent. He didn't allow my roots to become weakened because I stood on the strength of His Word. Yes, there were seasons I felt my roots would wither and die and that I would never bear the fruits that God intended for me to bear, but in every circumstance and in every situation, He caused me to triumph and has manifested landslide victories for His glory!

What I've always longed for was never far away, it just lay dormant inside of me until I could truly seek to discover *me*. Symbolically speaking, the tree and the stages of growth it has to endure to become useful, expresses the essence of *me*. Through each phase the tree is learning its capabilities as well as its limitations and completes a journey of self-discovery. This complicated, yet beautiful journey of me has taught me that treasures truly are hidden in earthen vessels and that with a lot of care, nourishment and time, the manifestations of fruits will be borne for all to see.

Useful for someone else's growth, our fruit should remain as Jesus commanded them to. Through this, people will see and know that a bountiful harvest awaits them as well when they commit to the work of finding the seed of life embedded within them. The oak tree in all of its glory has a defined strength to be envied, but the palm tree remains flexible when the storms of life unexpectedly showers down. BE the oak in your heart, but DISPLAY characteristics of the palm in your spirit. Always be open to how and what the Spirit is leading you into on your journey---the destination will be well worth it.

Life's obstacles attempted to dictate the quality of life I would have and tried to take away all the reasons to celebrate the victory of overcoming birth complications, abandonment issues, molestation from relatives and family friends, sexual abuse at the hands of both males and females, the silencing of my God-given voice and savagely executing my dreams, teenage pregnancies, persecution from the Church, ridicule, embarrassment, shame, depression, emotional, physical and psychological abuse, worthlessness, near-death experiences, broken marriage, mistreatment, infidelity, neglect, significant deaths, bankruptcy, and foreclosure. But it didn't, because God never allowed its limited strength to overtake nor overshadow the greatness of His!

As in the story of the Prodigal Son, I too had to peruse the scenic route through detours of riotous living and the misguiding of ill-intended companions. During a period of hardship, the Bible records the account that this son had "come to himself" and when he'd recognized the error of his ways, he humbled himself, remembered his loving father and returned home. He re-wrote the ending to his initially wretched story and suddenly just as quickly as he had ventured into dangerously unchartered territories there was a marked turnaround that enabled him to walk into the greatest form of himself that catapulted him into his greatest level of destiny. He had been restored! And although others couldn't understand the grace that was administered to him while he was outside the ark of safety, it did not negate the fact that the Father's love for his son is what claimed the victory at the end of the day. Eternally, the Prodigal Son has given hope to those of us who during life's twists and turns became self-sufficient, self-reliant and lost our way. There remains a loving Father who waits on us to come home so that our celebration can officially begin and be seen by all, even the ones who are resentful of our safe return.

The Prodigal Son came to himself and found destiny. I came to myself and re-discovered my voice! Though the enemy consistently strove to snuff it out, crush it and kill it, my voice survived every damaged, deliberate, deadly attack and powerfully emerged from the depths of Hell and is distinctly recognized and heard!

Just as Jesus rose on the third day following His crucifixion after snatching back the keys of death, hell, and the grave from the enemy of our souls, so my voice has risen to declare God's glory on the Earth! Excited over the fact that I serve a full-circle God that causes all things to work out together for the good of them who loves Him, when enough became enough and I, fully armored with spiritual warfare gear, decided to step in the ring of my own life, I quickly realized that I don't fight alone, God fights for me!

Every battle He's already claimed as His own because He causes me triumph and makes me win! I am an overcomer and as you climb the steep, rocky paths of this life, utilizing the tools within you, you will find that you are an overcomer too. The journey begins within! There's a *you* that's waiting on you. Seek, and you shall find; knock, and the doors that hold the answers will fling open unto you. Though you may suffer persecution along the way, remain encouraged to know that you will never be forsaken. Pursue and Triumph!

Signed,

A Survivor

About the Author

Born in Raleigh NC, Onica Michelle Royal grew up all of her life as a "PK" (Preacher's Kid) under the leadership of her late father and Pastor, Bishop Randy B. Royal.

Although surrounded by a family fully immersed in ministry, life for her still proved to be very rocky and tumultuous. Graced by God, her firm foundation of faith was laid in part by her grandmother, Sarah Louise Royal who imparted invaluable lessons of life by example and through demonstration.

Called into ministry, Onica has used this vein to be impactful in both secular and spiritual arenas. Her educational background consist of a Bachelor of Social Work from Barton College along with degrees in Human Services and Theological Studies. She is currently pursuing studies in Christian Counseling and seeks to assist the Kingdom in becoming healed and whole.

www.ingramcontent.com/pod-product-compliance
Lightning Source LLC
Chambersburg PA
CBHW071410290426
44108CB00014B/1757